STUDIES IN THE UK ECONOMY

UK industrialization and deindustrialization

Third edition

Stephen Bazen
University of Bordeaux

Tony Thirlwall
University of Kent at Canterbury

Series Editor
Bryan Hurl
Harrow School

Heinemann

Heinemann Educational Publishers
Halley Court, Jordan Hill, Oxford OX2 8EJ
a division of Reed Educational & Professional Publishing Ltd

OXFORD FLORENCE PRAGUE MADRID ATHENS
MELBOURNE AUCKLAND KUALA LUMPUR SINGAPORE TOKYO
IBADAN NAIROBI KAMPALA JOHANNESBURG GABORONE
PORTSMOUTH, NH CHICAGO MEXICO CITY SÃO PAULO

First published 1989 as *Deindustrialization*
Third edition published 1997

01 00 99 98 97
10 9 8 7 6 5 4 3 2 1

British Library Cataloguing in Publication Data
A catalogue record for this book is available from the British Library

ISBN 0 435 33039 X

Typeset and illustrated by TechType, Abingdon, Oxon.
Printed and bound in Great Britain by Biddles Ltd, Guildford

Acknowledgements

The Publishers would like to thank the following for permission to
reproduce copyright material:

The Associated Examining Board for the question on p. 71; © *The Economist*,
London 19.3.94 on p. 29, 15.6.96 on p. 38, 6–12.8.94 on pp. 40–41 and 8.6.96 on p.
75; London Examinations, A divisions of Edexcel Foundation for the questions on pp.
40, 57, 58–9 and 71; The *Financial Times* for 'The ills of manufacturing', by M. Wolf,
14-5-96 on p. 70; *The Guardian* for a table and figure on p. 58, for the article 'North
fights back in Swan crisis', by M. Hasall on pp. 73–74 and for the article 'One last
chance for manufacturing', by S. Beavis on pp. 85–6; Northern Examinations and
Assessment Board for the question on pp. 39–40; The *Observer* for the article
'Incredible shrinking Britain', by M. Kitson and J. Michie on p. 55; the OECD for the
tables on p. 17; table and charts from the *Employment Gazette* (now *Labour Market
Trends*) on pp. 22 and 27 and table from *Annual Abstract of Statistics* on p. 67 Crown
Copyright. Reproduced by permission of the Controller of HMSO and of the Office of
National Statistics; Oxford and Cambridge Examinations and Assessment Council for
the questions on pp. 26, 57 and 85; table 2.3 from *British Economic Growth* by
Crafts by permission of Oxford University Press on p. 13; Ingram Pinn/*Financial
Times* for the cartoon on p. 90; Routledge for the extract from *The age of
manufactures* by Maxine Burg on p. 13; 'Naked truth on investment', by M. Taylor
reproduced by kind permission of Mark Taylor, Fellow in Economics, University
College, Oxford on p. 47; © Times Newspapers Limited for the article 'Britain
tumbles down the competition league table' and the accompanying table by Philip
Bassett from the *Times*, 16.5.95 on pp. 76–7; University of Cambridge Local
Examinations Syndicate for the questions on pp. 12, 13–14, 26–7, 40–41, 57, 71–3
and 85–7.

The publishers have made every effort to contact the correct copyright holders.
However, if any material has been incorrectly acknowledged, the publishers will be
pleased to make the necessary arrangements at the earliest opportunity.

Contents

Preface

The first two editions of this book were called simply *Deindustrialization*. The expanded title of this third edition emphasizes that the book is now appropriate for the study of the UCLES Modular A level Paper 4383.

However, suitably updated and in some cases refocussed, it is also a source that is essential for this important topic as it appears in other exam papers at A and AS level.

Bryan Hurl
Series Editor

Introduction

'Alice thought "It's sure to make some change in my size; and as it can't possibly make me larger, it must make me smaller, I suppose?"'
Lewis Carroll

The subject matter of the phenomenon of deindustrialization is a very important one, and a very topical one in the United Kingdom economy. Compared with what has been happening in other countries the process in the UK seems to have been severe, particularly in terms of the fall in the share of industrial output in total output and the loss of jobs in manufacturing industry. This affects all our lives, either directly or indirectly.

If employment or output in industry declines, this has implications for:

* the overall level of employment and unemployment;
* the rate of growth of output (i.e. gross domestic product or GDP);
* the economy's balance of payments position if exports and imports are dominated by manufactured goods.

All this has further implications for a country's exchange rate, for its rate of interest, and for the whole of economic policy. To study deindustrialization, its causes and its consequences, involves a consideration of both microeconomic and macroeconomic issues.

In *Chapter 1* we consider how the economic structure of a country evolves through time as countries get richer, and the conditions necessary for industrialization to occur, using Rostow's stage theory of economic development and the experience of Britain's industrial revolution.

In *Chapter 2* we discuss the meaning of deindustrialization, and the extent of deindustrialization within the UK and in comparison with other countries.

Chapter 3 focuses on the question of whether deindustrialization matters. Some say it doesn't, but we argue that it does because it can be a major cause of unemployment; it can adversely affect a country's growth potential, and it can seriously damage a country's balance of payments unless other tradeable activities can compensate.

Chapter 4 examines the causes of deindustrialization. We discuss a number of hypotheses, including technical progress; crowding-out by government; the impact of North Sea oil in the 1980s; underinvestment in manufacturing, and the UK's weak trading performance.

Chapter 5 concentrates explicitly on the collapse of the manufacturing sector since 1979, including analysis of the two deep recessions, 1979–82 and 1990–92.

In *Chapter 6* the policy implications of our analysis are contemplated, and what the future holds, particularly as Europe becomes ever more integrated, and competition in industrial goods intensifies from other parts of the world.

* How can competitiveness be improved?
* Is there a role for protection?
* Does the 'single market' and further European integration threaten UK industry?
* How would a single currency affect the deindustrialization process?
* What are the implications for the economy of greater reliance on investment from overseas?

The *Conclusion* gives a summary of the arguments.

Chapter One

Industrialization

'God did not endow any country with the natural ability to produce industrial goods.'

===

Economic sectors

In discussing and analysing the evolution and growth of economies, it is common to distinguish between three major types of economic activity - agriculture, industry and services. These are sometimes also referred to as the primary, secondary, and tertiary sectors, respectively, although the correspondence is not always exact.

- The **primary sector** is land-based and therefore includes mining as well as agriculture.
- The **secondary sector** includes not only manufacturing, but also associated activities such as construction, transport and public utilities.
- The **tertiary sector** covers a wide spectrum ranging from the 'output' of hairdressers to the performance of opera at Covent Garden and work done by economists in Her Majesty's Treasury.

Looking at countries over time, or looking across different countries at a point in time, the relative importance of these activities is seen to differ enormously in terms of their contribution to total output (or GDP) and employment.

Table 1 shows the share of agriculture, industry and services in total output for three groups of countries in the world economy classified by the World Bank into low-income, middle-income, and high-income countries.

The **low-income countries** are the less developed countries of Asia, Africa and Latin America with a *per capita* income of less than $800 a year. The middle-income countries are the newly industrializing countries in Asia, Latin America and Eastern Europe with *per capita* incomes between $800 and $9000. The **high-income countries** are the developed industrialized nations of Europe, North America, Japan, and a handful of other countries with *per capita* incomes in excess of $9000. The shares of output are given for two dates, 1970 and 1993.

Table 1 Share of total output by sector (per cent)

Country	Agriculture		Industry		Services	
	1970	1993	1970	1993	1970	1993
Low-income	37	28	28	35	35	37
Middle-income	18	12	34	37	48	51
High-income	4	4	44	41	52	55
United Kingdom	3	2	45	33	52	65

In general terms it can be seen that there is a broad shift from agriculture to industry to services as countries become richer, although exceptions can be found to this rule.

In 1970, the share of agriculture in total output in the low-income countries was 37 per cent compared with 4 per cent in the high-income countries, but even in low-income countries it had declined to 28 per cent in 1993. At the same time, the share of industry in total output in low-income countries was only 28 per cent compared with 44 per cent in high-income countries, but the share rose to 35 per cent in 1993. In the UK the current distribution of output is: agriculture 2 per cent; industry 33 per cent; services 65 per cent.

The distribution of employment will mirror the distribution of output, although not exactly, because the productivity of labour differs both between sectors, and within sectors between countries. In general, labour productivity is lower in agriculture and services than in industry, and this difference is more marked the poorer the country. This means that agriculture's share of total employment will tend to be higher than its share of total output; and the more so, the poorer the country.

For example, while the share of agriculture in total output in low-income countries in 1993 was 28 per cent, the share of employment in agriculture was over 50 per cent. By comparison, the share of industry in total output in high-income countries in 1993 was 41 per cent, while the share of employment in industry was only 25 per cent. In the UK the share of employment in agriculture fell from 36 per cent in 1801 to 2 per cent in 1993, while the share in industry rose from 30 per cent in 1801 to a peak of 47.7 per cent in 1961, and is now only 25 per cent. The share of employment in services of all kinds rose from 34 per cent to over 70 per cent in 1993.

Stages of development

There are three basic factors to account for the structure of output and employment within countries, and why it changes through time:

- the stage of development reached by a country;
- foreign trade;
- the stage of the business cycle, since some activities are more cyclical than others.

By far the most important determinant of economic structure is the stage of development. The American economic historian, **W.W. Rostow**, has developed a theory of the stages of growth that helps to explain the changing structure of output and employment in the course of development, and the processes of industrialization and deindustrialization that we are concerned with in this book. He identifies *five stages of economic growth and development*, each with its own characteristics, which he calls:

1. the traditional stage;
2. the transitional stage;
3. take-off;
4. maturity;
5. the stage of high mass consumption.

• The traditional stage

All societies were once at subsistence level with people eking out a living by hunting, fishing and growing subsistence crops. These economies were exclusively primary, generating output and income from land-based activities. They correspond to Rostow's **traditional stage** where there is no industry, technology is minimal, and the economies are essentially stagnant ('pre-Newtonian' as Rostow describes them).

A precondition for any other form of activity to take place is that individuals within a society must be able to produce more than a means of subsistence for themselves so that time is made available to engage in other activities and a food surplus exists to feed people engaged in non-agricultural pursuits.

• The transitional stage

Historically, the basis for the diversification of economic activities was when farmers were able to devote effort to the improvement of the land and to apply technology to agriculture to raise productivity, which is the essential requirement for the generation of a surplus of agricultural goods over subsistence needs. This is the stage of development that Rostow refers to as the **transitional stage**, in which the conditions are laid for economic progress and eventually take-off into self-sustaining growth when the importance of industry in the total economy increases dramatically.

The agricultural sector has three main roles to play in the industrialization process.

- The agricultural surplus provides the food for those who work in industrial activities.
- The industrial workforce must come from agriculture.
- Saving from the sale of surplus production in agriculture can provide the investment resources for industry.

In this transitional phase, the growth of output must exceed the growth of population so that there is a continued increase in *per capita* income and saving. Investment must also rise and be devoted to improving the means of transport and other social overhead capital to build up society's infrastructure. A capitalist class must emerge, to supersede in authority the land-based elite of the traditional society, willing to take risks and respond to material incentives. The foundations are then laid for industrialization to take place.

Today, in many poor, or less developed, countries, still over 50 per cent of output and 70 per cent of employment is accounted for by primary, land-based activities. In the so-called developed countries of Europe and North America, the situation is very different with not more than 10 per cent of resources devoted to primary production. The explanation is that the now-developed countries experienced the transitional stage of development much earlier, way back in the seventeenth and eighteenth centuries, characterized particularly by a revolution in agricultural productivity and improvements in transport. Many of today's less developed countries are still in the transitional stage and have yet to experience a marked improvement in agricultural productivity.

- Take-off

Once an agricultural revolution has taken place, and the other conditions in the transitional stage have been met, then industry can 'take-off'.

The UK's industrial revolution of the late eighteenth and early nineteenth centuries was the first example in the world of successful industrial take-off (see below). Its major distinguishing feature was the widespread application of machinery to the production of goods within the context of a factory system, enabling the mass production of goods within a disciplined work environment. The gains in productivity and living standards were enormous, although the working conditions were invariably harsh.

Some less developed countries are now experiencing a similar industrial transformation – the so-called newly industrializing countries

(NICs) in South-East Asia and Latin America.

The take-off stage of industrialization is usually relatively short, but to be successful it is essential for 'leading growth sectors' to emerge, particularly with the ability to export in order to pay for the import requirements for growth. In the UK's **industrial revolution**, textiles and engineering were two leading sectors.

For take-off not to be abortive, there must also exist a political, social and institutional framework conducive to industrial expansion, such as adequate finance and credit mechanisms, and a legal system able to enforce contracts.

- ## Maturity

Following take-off, there is the stage of **maturity** in which society has effectively applied the range of known technology to the bulk of resources, so that levels of productivity are roughly equal across sectors.

New leading sectors replace the old, and accompanying changes in industrial structure will be structural changes in society at large, such as an increase in the number of white-collar workers, a switch in industrial leadership from the entrepreneur to the manager, and the growth of demand for services – some a function of increases in leisure time which accompany increased labour productivity. In the maturity phase the growth of industry slows down, and industry is likely to be overtaken in importance by service activities.

Services cover a wide spectrum. Typically, the first types of services to emerge in an agricultural economy are related to marketing and dis-tribution. Farmers want to sell their produce, so that markets develop. With the establishment of markets come merchants, wholesalers and retailers – intermediaries between producers and consumers. Mar-keting, in turn, requires transport provision. Surplus agricultural output, and the industrial activities it permits, will also give rise to the demand for personal services, as well as banking and insurance.

In addition, societies will witness the collective provision of services as the scope of government expands to provide law and order, defence, health, education, and so on.

As development proceeds a whole variety of services spring up, ran-ging in sophistication according to the level of development. In capitalist economies, banking and financial services develop in profu-sion as business grows and the demand for capital and finance expands. As markets develop in financial assets, more resources are devoted to the exchange of these assets in secondary markets. This is well illustrated by the growth and dominance of the City of London in the British economy.

• **High mass consumption**

The consumption of services is very much the distinguishing feature of Rostow's final stage of development, the stage of **high mass consumption**. In terms of the proportion of resources devoted to service activities, the provision of basic services such as distribution and transport first grows and then declines, but the provision of more sophisticated services, associated with financial services, leisure and tourism, and high class retailing, grows and grows.

• **The overall picture**

In general, in the early stages of development, the proportion of resources devoted to both industry and services grows, while agriculture declines. In the later stages of development, agriculture continues to decline, services continue to grow, but the proportion of resources devoted to industry levels off and then starts to decline.

This proportionate decline may also be accompanied by an absolute decline in industrial employment, if not output. The process of industrialization gives way to the process of **deindustrialization**, which we describe in more detail in Chapter 2. A graphical summary of changes in the structure of production in the stages of development is given in Figure 1.

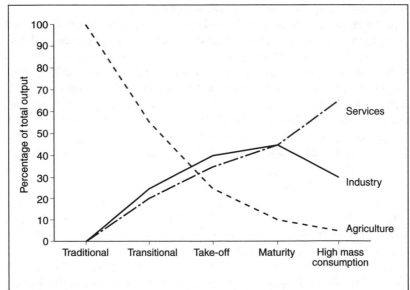

Figure 1 The structure of production in the stages of development

Britain's industrial revolution

A number of factors contributed to Britain being the first country in the world to experience an industrial revolution. Firstly, it was the first country in Europe to reform its agricultural sector through the abolition of serfdom and the enclosure movement which raised agricultural productivity and provided surplus labour and food to support industrial expansion. Secondly, there was an outburst of inventive genius in the eighteenth century. The inventiveness of its people provided the first steam engine (James Watt) and machinery capable of mass production (Kay's flying shuttle and Arkwright's spinning jenny). The industrial revolution started in the spinning of cotton and spread to other branches of textiles and then to other industries which adopted mechanization and the factory system of mass production which lowered costs and prices. Thirdly, Britain possessed abundant supplies of water, wood and coal as sources of fuel and power. Fourthly, even before the invention of the railways in the 1820s, which greatly accelerated the pace of industrialization, Britain possessed a unique system of canals and rivers for the easy transportation of goods and raw materials, which was also helped by the fact that Britain was a unified nation with no barriers to trade between regions, unlike some continental countries. Finally, Britain was not ravaged by war, and already had strong trading links with America and the East which provided ready markets for newly produced goods. In 1700, the number employed in industry was only 5 per cent of the workforce or 200 000 people. By 1800, this had risen to 3 million, and to 6 million by 1900, or 46 per cent of the workforce.

Britain remained the workshop of the world until the advent of a second industrial revolution in the 1870s based on steel and electricity, when Germany and the United States, in particular, challenged Britain's pre-eminence – and later Russia, France and Italy. In all these countries, railways spread, and the production of coal, iron and steel, chemicals, and then electricity, increased rapidly.

The income elasticity of demand

It is important to understand that the shifts in the structure of production described earlier, between primary, secondary and tertiary activities, are related to the important concept in economics known as the **income elasticity of demand.**

The income elasticity of demand for a product is measured by the percentage change in quantity demanded divided by the percentage change in income. If the income elasticity of demand is less than one (unity), this means that as income grows, the demand for a product

9

grows less than in proportion, so the share of income devoted to the purchase of that product falls. By comparison, if the income elasticity is greater than one, the share of income devoted to the purchase of that product rises. If the income elasticity is exactly one, the share stays the same.

- The income elasticity of demand for agricultural goods and primary products is typically less than one (known as **Engel's Law**). That is why the share of agricultural output in total output is observed to fall as countries get richer; there is an obvious limit to the amount of food people can consume.
- The income elasticity of demand for most industrial goods and service activities is greater than one. That is why the share of industry and services in total output is observed to rise as countries progress in the early and middle stages of development.

But the income elasticity of demand for sophisticated services is greater than for manufactured goods in the later stages of development, and that is why the relative importance of service activities continues to rise, while that of industry levels off and even falls.

Foreign trade

The stage of development of a country will determine the long-run division of output between agriculture, industry and services. But superimposed on the long-run structural trend described above will be other forces determining the pattern of production, one of which will be the structure of foreign trade.

Countries are differently endowed with resources, which means that they have a different **comparative advantage** in the production of certain goods. That is, the opportunity cost of producing a particular good will be cheaper than for another. According to the law of comparative advantage (first developed by the English classical economist David Ricardo) it will pay a country to specialize in that good and to trade it for other goods it wants, rather than attempting to be self-sufficient. Thus, if a country has a comparative advantage in agriculture, and it decides to specialize in agriculture (or has no effective choice), this will keep resources in agriculture even though there is an internal shift in demand away from primary products, because the income elasticity of demand is less than one.

This helps to explain why countries at the same level of *per capita* income may still have quite large differences in the proportion of resources devoted to agriculture and other primary commodities. Likewise, if a country acquires a comparative advantage in industry, this will tend to reinforce a 'natural' industrialization process in the early stages of development, and may accelerate the shift of resources from agriculture and delay the shift of resources into services.

Fierce competition in trade, however, may erode a country's comparative advantage, particularly in the field of industrial goods, and this will tend to accelerate the demise of industry and accelerate the shift of resources into services. (The shift must be into tradeable services, however, if balance of payments problems are not to arise; see Chapter 3.)

In discussing comparative advantage and trade, and the effect this has on the structure of production and economic performance, it must be remembered that comparative advantage is not a natural phenomenon except in the field of primary production. *God did not endow any economy with the natural ability to produce industrial goods.* In these goods, comparative advantage is *acquired*, and was acquired sooner in some countries than others. This is the basic explanation for the **north–south divide** in the world economy, between the primary-producing less developed economies of the 'south', on the one hand, and the industrialized developed economies of the 'north' on the other.

It is an interesting question, which goes beyond the scope of this book, of how less developed countries might foster structural change to reduce dependence on primary products and accelerate the process of industrialization.

The business cycle

Some activities are subject to greater cyclical fluctuations than others, and this will cause temporary disturbances to the sectoral ratios of output and employment.

Primary commodities can be subject to severe **supply shocks**, associated with weather conditions and harvest failures, as well as **demand shocks** due to world recession. In comparison, industrial output suffers mainly from demand shocks emanating both from within the country and from outside. Service activities, taken as a whole, tend to be the most cyclically stable.

It is difficult to say anything categoric on this issue except that it is possible for the long-run trend in structural change to have cyclical fluctuations superimposed upon it, which may affect calculations of the degree of industrialization or deindustrialization being experienced, depending on the starting date and terminal date of the analysis. If the base year taken is the height of a boom and the terminal year is the bottom of a recession, the process of industrialization may look weaker than it is and the extent of deindustrialization may look more serious than the true underlying trend would indicate.

This is well illustrated in the UK economy in the 1980s and 90s when two severe cyclical downturns in the economy (and other factors) induced a massive loss of jobs in manufacturing industry in excess of the underlying structural loss. Some of the cyclical loss was then recovered in the subsequent booms, as Chapter 5 describes.

KEY WORDS

Primary sector	Industrial revolution
Secondary sector	Maturity
Tertiary sector	High mass consumption
Low-income countries	Deindustrialization
Middle-income countries	Income elasticity of demand
High-income countries	Engel's Law
Rostow	Comparative advantage
Traditional stage	North–south divide
Transitional stage	Supply shocks
Take-off	Demand shocks

Reading list
Rostow, W.W., *The Stages of Economic Growth*, Cambridge University Press, 1960.

Essay topics
1 (a) Why was the British economy the first one to 'take-off' into self-sustained economic growth in the second half of the eighteenth century? [12 marks]
   (b) Assess the impact of industrialization on employment in the UK economy. [8 marks]
   [University of Cambridge Local Examinations Syndicate 1996]
2 (a) Explain how industrialization had affected the structure of the British economy by the middle of the nineteenth century. [10 marks]
   (b) Discuss the costs and benefits of this industrialization for British workers. [10 marks]
   [University of Cambridge Local Examinations Syndicate 1997]

Data Response Question

This task is based on a question set by the University of Cambridge Local Examinations Syndicate in 1996. Study the following information and then answer the questions.

The period of the mid-eighteenth century to the middle of the nineteenth century has often been described as a period of 'industrial revolution'. This view is no longer held by many economic historians, who describe it more as a period of gradual change in most industries and a period of spectacular change in a few high-profile industries. The former industries experienced what is often referred to as 'learning by doing' improvements rather than great breakthroughs; in the second group of industries there were important new developments which were responsible for their substantial increase in output.

© Maxine Berg, *The Age of Manufactures*, Routledge

Table 1 shows the 'value added' in various industries from 1770 to 1831; Figure 1 shows the growth in real output for all manufacturing industries over the period 1700 to 1850.

Table 1 Value added in British industry (£m, current)

	1770	%	1801	%	1831	%
Cotton	0.6	(2.6)	9.2	(17.0)	25.3	(22.4)
Wool	7.0	(30.5)	10.1	(18.7)	15.9	(14.1)
Linen	1.9	(8.3)	2.6	(4.8)	5.0	(4.4)
Silk	1.0	(4.4)	2.0	(3.7)	5.8	(5.1)
Building	2.4	(10.5)	9.3	(17.2)	26.5	(23.4)
Iron	1.5	(6.6)	4.0	(7.4)	7.6	(6.7)
Copper	0.2	(0.9)	0.9	(1.7)	0.8	(0.7)
Beer	1.3	(5.7)	2.5	(4.6)	5.2	(4.6)
Leather	5.1	(22.2)	8.4	(15.5)	9.8	(8.7)
Soap	0.3	(1.3)	0.8	(1.5)	1.2	(1.1)
Candles	0.5	(2.2)	1.0	(1.8)	1.2	(1.1)
Coal	0.9	(4.4)	2.7	(5.0)	7.9	(7.0)
Paper	0.1	(0.4)	0.6	(1.1)	0.8	(0.7)
	22.8		54.1		113.0	

Source: Crafts, *British Economic Growth*, table 2.3

Figure 1 Trend growth of industry

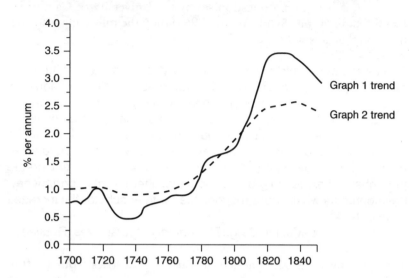

Adapted from: Crafts, Leybourne and Mills, 'Britain', pp. 132 and 140.

Graph 1 represents the trend growth of Craft's complete industry sample.

Graph 2 represents the trend growth of Craft's industry sample excluding cotton, iron, steel and coal.

1. (a) Explain what is meant by 'value added'. [2 marks]
   (b) Which industry experienced the greatest decrease in its (relative) share of output between 1770 and 1831? [1 mark]
2. (a) How far does the data in Table 1 give a realistic picture of the distribution of occupational employment in the UK in 1770? [2 marks]
   (b) How could the trends shown in Table 1 be related to the demographic change in this period? [2 marks]
3. (a) Describe the trend in total industrial production shown in Graph 1 between 1750 and 1850. [1 mark]
   (b) How does this trend change when the cotton, iron, steel and coal industries are excluded? [2 marks]
   (c) State and explain two reasons which might account for this variation. [4 marks]
4. Discuss the likely impact of the output changes shown in Table 1 on the organization and structure of British industry. [6 marks]

Chapter Two

The meaning and extent of deindustrialization

'Deindustrialization has gatecrashed the literature, thereby avoiding the entrance fee of a definition.' Frank Blackaby

Defining deindustrialization

The term deindustrialization refers to a long-term contraction of the manufacturing sector. Some commentators also include in this mining and quarrying, gas, electricity and water, and construction. How it should be measured is a source of disagreement.

What is needed is an operational definition which gauges the seriousness of the decline of the manufacturing sector. It should be *cause-free* in the sense that it should not prejudge the cause(s). Some definitions of deindustrialization do prejudge the cause(s), rather as the definition of inflation as 'too much money chasing too few goods' prejudges the cause of inflation, and therefore precludes wider analysis.

An operational definition should also possess *universality*. This means it should be neither time-specific nor place-specific, and it should be easily observable and permit international comparisons. Two definitions which satisfy these criteria are:

- a declining share of total employment in manufacturing;
- an absolute decline in employment in manufacturing.

Interpreting employment trends

To understand what is happening to the numbers employed in industry and to the share of **industrial employment** in total employment, it is important for students to understand some simple concepts:

- Output, O, is equal to the product of the level of employment, E, and the productivity of labour, O/E. That is, $O \equiv E \times (O/E)$.
- It follows from the above identity that the **growth of output**, o, is the sum of the growth of employment, e, and the growth of **labour productivity**, p. That is, $o = e + p$. Hence the growth of employment can be written as equal to the difference between the growth of output and the growth of labour productivity, so that $e = o - p$. It will be remembered from Chapter 1 that output will grow at different

rates in different sectors according to the income elasticity of demand for output.

- If the growth of employment in a sector is greater than the total growth of employment in the economy, the share of employment in that sector will rise, and vice versa. Employment shifts out of agriculture relatively and absolutely since the growth of output is low relative to productivity growth (in agriculture). Employment shifts into services relatively and absolutely since output growth is high relative to productivity growth (in services). The income elasticity of demand for services is high and productivity growth in services is typically slow.

As far as industry is concerned, there are four possibilities:

1. The share of employment could be rising and the absolute number employed in industry could be rising if industrial employment is growing faster than total employment and output growth in industry is faster than productivity growth. This is the case in the early stages of industrialization and during take-off.
2. The share of employment could be rising and the absolute numbers falling. This is highly unlikely, however, because if industrial employment is growing faster than total employment, output growth in industry is also likely to be rapid and to exceed productivity growth.
3. The share of employment could be falling and the absolute numbers rising. This is typical in the later stages of industrialization, during Rostow's maturity phase.
4. The share of employment could be falling and the absolute numbers falling because employment growth in industry is slower than total employment growth, and output growth in industry is slow relative to productivity growth. This is a phenomenon in some of the more 'decadent' industrial economies including the UK, as we shall come to see.

Table 2 shows that most developed economies have experienced a declining share of civilian employment in the manufacturing sector since 1960, and Table 3 shows a falling share of output relative to GDP. However this may not reflect an absolute contraction of the manufacturing sector.

Table 2 The share of manufacturing as a percentage of total civilian employment in certain OECD countries (OECD data) (%)

	1960	*1970*	*1979*	*1992*
UK	36.0	34.5	29.3	20.8
Canada	23.7	22.3	19.9	17.0
USA	27.1	26.4	22.7	18.5
Japan	21.5	27.0	24.3	24.2
France	27.5	27.8	26.1	21.3
Germany	37.0	39.4	34.3	31.6
Italy	23.0	27.8	26.7	22.7
Netherlands	30.6	26.4	22.3	19.0
Norway	25.3	26.7	20.5	15.8

Table 3 The share of manufacturing as a percentage of total output in certain OECD countries (OECD data) (%)

	1960	*1970*	*1979*	*1992*
UK	32.1	28.1	24.9	19.3
Canada	23.3	20.4	19.1	16.0*
USA	28.6	25.7	23.8	19.3
Japan	33.9	35.9	30.1	27.1
France	29.1	28.7	27.0	20.4
Germany	40.3	38.2	34.1	28.7
Italy	28.5	28.9	30.6	20.5
Netherlands	33.6	28.2	19.0	18.3
Norway	21.3	21.8	18.2	13.5†

*1990; †1991

If a falling share is simply the result of employment in manufacturing growing at a slower rate than total employment, deindustrialization may not be a cause for concern. A declining share of employment might be expected in the process of development as the composition of demand shifts away from manufactured goods towards service-type activities, including leisure pursuits and foreign travel.

On the other hand, an absolute decline in manufacturing employment is a cause for concern, and this will also mean a declining share of manufacturing employment if employment in other sectors is growing, or contracting at a slower rate.

In fact, the only situation in which an absolute decline in employment in manufacturing might provide a misleading picture of the health of the economy is if technology is expanding very rapidly so that labour productivity is also expanding very rapidly, leading to falls in employment. However, as we argue below, technical progress should not be the enemy of employment in the long run since technical progress creates new products, new wants and new manufacturing industries – at least it has done so historically. Technical progress and productivity growth are also vital for countries to remain competitive in the world economy, without which the demand for exports will fall and make employment worse. *This consideration gives rise to a distinction in the literature between positive and negative deindustrialization.*

Positive and negative deindustrialization

Employment in manufacturing declines when the rate of growth of output is lower than the rate of growth of labour productivity. If employment is falling because a high rate of growth of output is being outstripped by an even higher rate of growth of labour productivity, then it is difficult to regard this decline as a cause for concern. Indeed it may be thought desirable that the number of hours worked per week, weeks worked per year, and the length of one's working life should fall secularly as the economy moves into the post-industrial stage. This is **positive deindustrialization.**

However, if it is a low growth of output that is being exceeded by a mediocre rate of growth of labour productivity, then the decline of employment is attributable to a sluggish growth of output, and the wealth to finance increased leisure time is not being created. The country is likely to be getting relatively poorer compared with other countries. This is **negative deindustrialization.**

- Thus positive deindustrialization occurs when the share of employment in manufacturing falls because of rapid productivity growth, but where displaced labour is absorbed into the non-manufacturing sector. The economy remains at full-employment and GDP *per capita* is higher.
- On the other hand, negative deindustrialization results from a decline in the share of manufacturing in total employment, owing to a slow growth or decline in demand for manufacturing output, and where displaced labour results in unemployment rather than being absorbed into the non-manufacturing sector. Here the fall in manufacturing employment is associated with stagnation and unemployment.

Deindustrialization can therefore be associated with *benefits* if accompanied by fast output growth, or cause *severe problems* if it is associated with stagnant output. When we come to examine the performance of the manufacturing sector in the UK, we shall see that the deindustrialization experienced has been predominantly of the negative kind.

The extent of deindustrialization

In this book we define and discuss deindustrialization as a long-term absolute decline in employment in the manufacturing sector. Figure 2 shows the long-term decline of manufacturing employment in the UK along with trends in the service sector (including Public Administration) and in total employment for the period 1966–94.

- Since 1966, employment in manufacturing has followed a relentless downward trend. Between 1966 and 1979, just over 2 million jobs were lost in manufacturing and a further 3 million were lost between 1979 and 1994.
- Employment in services grew rapidly between 1970 and 1980 – some 2.3 million jobs were created in net terms – after a period of relatively slow growth in the 1960s.
- Total employment (excluding the self-employed and the armed forces) fell after 1966 by 0.9 million up to 1972 and thereafter rose slightly, reaching a peak in 1979 and then fell dramatically in the recession of the early 1980s. Since then total employment has recovered owing to the growth in service sector employment, but it failed to return to its 1979 level before falling away again after 1990.

The overall picture, therefore, is one of a long-term decline in manufacturing employment which caused total employment to fall in the late 1960s, but this was counteracted by the growth of employment in services between 1972 and 1979. Between 1979 and 1983 manufacturing and total employment contracted together. After 1983 manufacturing employment continued to contract while the growth in service sector employment enabled total employment to expand. Manufacturing employment appeared to stabilize at the end of the 1980s but the recession of the early 1990s caused it to fall away again. Another 800 000 jobs were lost in manufacturing between 1989 and 1994. This contributed to the 1.3 million reduction in total employment – the other main sector affected being construction.

In the last twenty years, the UK economy has experienced two severe recessions, in 1979–83 and 1990–93. These severe shocks each added a large cyclical component to the underlying structural decline. On our definition of deindustrialization, it has been a continuous process since 1966, which was greatly exacerbated by the events of the late 1970s and early 1980s, and the early 1990s.

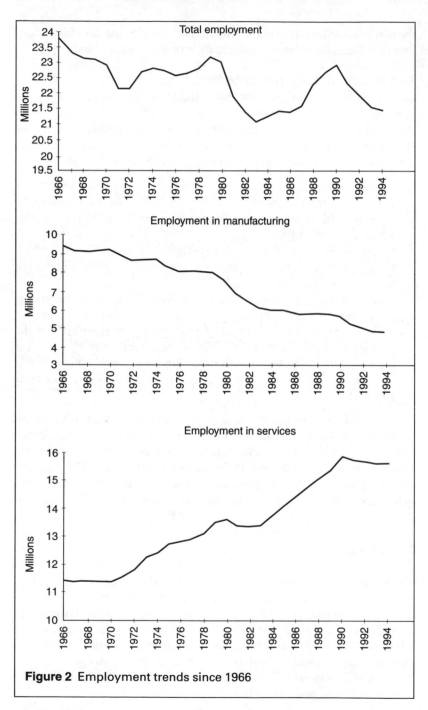

Figure 2 Employment trends since 1966

Manufacturing employment by industry

Given the extent of the contraction of manufacturing employment, it is important to see whether it has been the result of the decline of one or two major industries within the manufacturing sector, or whether it has been a widespread phenomenon across all industries.

Table 4 shows changes in the absolute level of employment over the period 1972–95, which is the longest run of figures available using the 1980 Standard Industrial Classification. Along with manufacturing as a whole, in the majority of industries employment peaked in the 1960s and there has been a relentless decline since then in all major activities. Particularly badly hit in the 1970s were 'Textiles, leather, footwear and clothing' and 'Metal manufacturing', with losses of 180 000 and 96 000 jobs, respectively, between 1972 and 1979. When the 1980s and 90s are taken into account, we find that these two sectors along with 'Motor vehicles and parts' and 'Other transport equipment' all experienced reductions in employment in excess of 50 per cent (between 1972 and 1995).

Manufacturing employment by region

The maps in Figure 3 show the **distribution of employment** in manufacturing across the eleven standard regions of the UK in 1966 and 1994.

The mass of manufacturing industry and employment is concentrated down a central axis running from the North West, through the West Midlands into the South East of England. These three regions contain around 50 per cent of manufacturing employment. Between 1966 and 1979 when manufacturing employment fell by 2 million, or nearly 20 per cent, all regions suffered except the South West and East Anglia. The worst-hit regions were the North West and the South East where manufacturing employment fell by 29.1 and 28.8 per cent, respectively.

- **The typically depressed regions**

Between 1979 and 1990, employment in manufacturing fell by a further 2 million, or nearly 30 per cent. Particularly badly hit during those 'Thatcher years' were not only Scotland, Northern Ireland, and the North and North West of England – the typically **depressed regions** of the UK – but also the West Midlands and the South East. In all these regions, manufacturing employment declined by over one-third.

Table 4 Employment in manufacturing in Great Britain* (thousands)

Standard Industrial Classification (1980)	1972	1979	1990	1995	% change 1972–95 (and absolute change)
Metal manufacturing	788	694	386	279	–64.6 (509)
Chemicals and artificial fibres	428	436	327	277	–35.3 (151)
Mechanical engineering	1057	1033	744	607	–42.6 (450)
Office machinery, electrical engineering and instruments	992	954	722	617	–37.6 (375)
Motor vehicles and parts	491	464	246	203	–58.7 (288)
Other transport equipment	403	376	243	160	–60.3 (243)
Metal goods not elsewhere specified	544	505	315	278	–48.9 (266)
Food, drink and tobacco	759	713	527	479	–36.9 (280)
Textiles, leather, footwear and clothing	986	800	478	424	–57.0 (562)
Timber, wooden furniture, rubber, plastics etc.	617	591	541	488	–20.9 (129)
Paper products, printing and publishing	558	542	483	459	–17.7 (99)

* Owing to changes in the Standard Industrial Classification, employment figures on a consistent basis over a long period are available only for Great Britain

Source: Department of Employment *Gazette* (various issues).

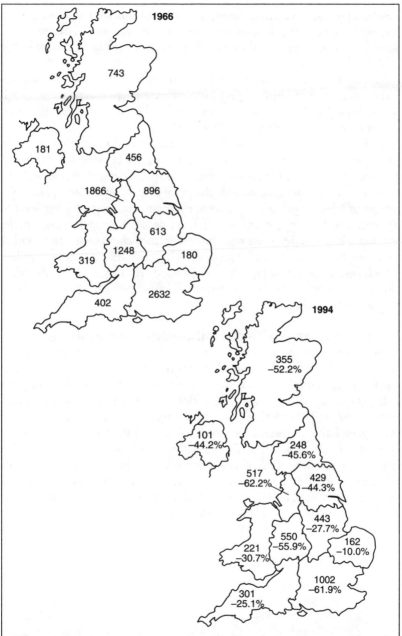

Figure 3 Employment in manufacturing by region (thousands), and the percentage decline

Although manufacturing employment fell in the 'south', it was offset by much higher employment growth in other sectors – particularly in services – which prevented unemployment from rising as fast as in the 'north'.

During the recession of the early 1990s, there were further substantial reductions in manufacturing employment particularly in the North West, West Midlands and the South East, where more than half a million jobs were lost between 1990 and 1995.

Regional disparities in employment growth and unemployment not only have welfare implications, but can also affect adversely the functioning of the overall economy. For example, demand pressure in the 'south' can affect wage inflation, the price of land and house prices, the effects of which 'spill over' into other regions, causing a higher level of aggregate inflation for any given level of aggregate demand in the economy as a whole. *Thus regional disparities can worsen the conflict between macroeconomic objectives.* Only an active regional policy which discriminates in favour of depressed regions, as far as the location of economic activity is concerned, can cope with these problems of regional imbalance.

Britain compared with other industrialized countries

If employment in manufacturing in the rest of the industrialized world has declined over a long period, the process of deindustrialization in the UK might simply be considered as part of a decreasingly important role played by manufacturing activities in the world economy at large.

However, as Table 5 shows, of the ten major advanced industrialized countries, half experienced an increase in manufacturing employment between 1960 and 1993. Furthermore, no country experienced a decline in employment of the proportion experienced by the UK, which saw employment in manufacturing fall by nearly 46 per cent over this period. The UK also experienced the largest proportionate decline in the period 1960–79. Although not alone in its experience, the UK is one of the few advanced industrialized countries to experience significant deindustrialization, and the process has been by far the most pronounced in the UK.

Table 5 Manufacturing employment in advanced industrialized countries 1960–1993 (thousands)

	1960	1979	Change 1960–79 (%)	1993	Change 1960–93 (%)
G7 countries					
USA	16 796	21 040	+25.3	17 965	+7.0
Canada	1 406*	2 047	+45.6	1 756	+24.9
Germany	(9 433)†	(8 370)	−11.3	9 092	−3.4
France	6 322	5 291	−16.3	4 192	−33.7
Italy	3 735‡	4 716‡	+26.3	4 609	+23.4
Japan	7 990	11 070	+38.5	15 637	+95.7
United Kingdom	8 996	7 253	−19.3	4 887	−45.6
Other EU countries					
Belgium	1 043	888	−14.9	873§	−16.3
Netherlands	1 082	(1037)	−4.2	932	−13.9
Spain	2 009	2 742	+36.5	2 553	+27.1
Sweden	1 499	1 359	−9.3	–	–

Wage and salary earners in the manufacturing sector unless otherwise specified. Figures in brackets are not strictly comparable with previous years.

* 1961; †1962; ‡Wage and salary earners in industry; §1992
Source: OECD

KEY WORDS

Industrial employment	Negative deindustrialization
Growth of output	Recessions
Labour productivity	Distribution of employment
Positive deindustrialization	Depressed regions

Reading list

Healey, N. and Cook, M., Chapter 2 in *Supply Side Economics,* 3rd edn, Heinemann Educational, 1996.

Maunders, P., et al, *Economics Explained,* 3rd edn, Collins Educational, 1996.

National Institute of Economic and Social Research (NIESR), Chapter 6 in *The UK Economy,* 3rd edn, Heinemann Educational, 1995.

Clark, A., Layard, R. and Rubin, M., *UK Unemployment,* 3rd edn, Heinemann Educational, 1997.

Essay topics

1. Explain clearly what is meant by the term 'deindustrialization'. Is the UK's experience of deindustrialization an inevitable feature of a mature economy? [20 marks]
   [University of Cambridge Local Examinations Syndicate, specimen paper, 1995]
2. Discuss the circumstances under which economists have argued that deindustrialization can produce net benefits to the UK economy. [20 marks]
   [Combined Boards of University of Cambridge Local Examinations Syndicate/Oxford and Cambridge Schools Examination Board, 1995]

Data Response Question

This task is based on a question set by the University of Cambridge Local Examinations Syndicate in 1996.

Since 1980 there has been a considerable change in the pattern of employment in the UK economy, with several leading economists expressing concern about the UK's manufacturing sector. There has been much interest in the growth of women's employment, and concern that women's part-time jobs may be replacing full-time jobs for men. Study Figures A to D and answer the questions below.

1. (a) Compare the trends in manufacturing and non-manufacturing employment during the period. [1 mark]
   (b) Discuss *two* possible economic consequences of this change in the pattern of employment. [4 marks]
2. (a) What happened to labour productivity in manufacturing industries between 1983 and 1990? Using the data, explain your reasoning. [2 marks]
   (b) Give *two* possible causes of changes in labour productivity. [2 marks]
3. To what extent does the information in Figure B support the view that women's part-time jobs are replacing male full-time jobs? [5 marks]
4. Assuming no increase in the level of population, discuss whether the data indicate an increase in the standard of living between 1983 and 1993. [6 marks]

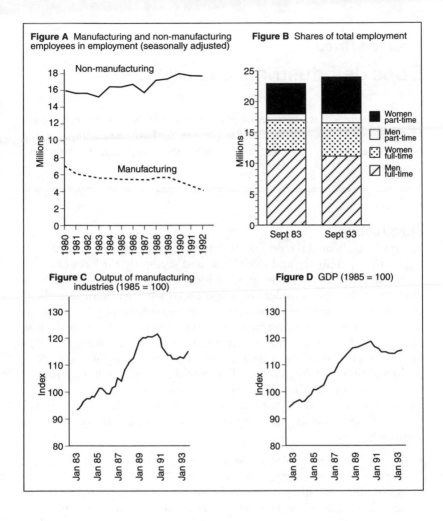

Figure A Manufacturing and non-manufacturing employees in employment (seasonally adjusted)

Figure B Shares of total employment

Figure C Output of manufacturing industries (1985 = 100)

Figure D GDP (1985 = 100)

Chapter Three
Does deindustrialization matter?

'I do not believe it is possible for Britain to trade its way into the future primarily as a service dominated economy ... A robust manufacturing base is a crucial element in a modern competitive economy.'
Tony Blair

Introduction
Having documented the decline of employment in the UK manufacturing sector by industry and by region, and seeing that it has generally been more pronounced than in other industrialized countries, it is now important that we consider the question of whether deindustrialization matters. Some commentators regard manufacturing as being no more and no less important than the service sector, and see the decline of the manufacturing sector as a normal feature of economic development, which should even be welcomed since office jobs are more congenial than factory jobs (see 'The manufacturing myth' opposite).

Here we outline three important reasons why a strong manufacturing sector may be both necessary and desirable for the overall health of the economy, and why service activities cannot be a perfect substitute.

- First, there are obvious implications for unemployment if the growth of the economy suffers.
- Secondly, it is widely recognized that the manufacturing sector has certain unique growth-inducing characteristics not found in other sectors of the economy.
- Thirdly, we emphasize the importance of manufacturing industry for a healthy balance of payments, and hence for the growth of the economy if it is not to be constrained by balance of payments deficits.

Historically, and up to as recently as 1982, the UK always had a surplus of trade in manufactured goods, which helped to pay for imports of food, raw materials and fuel. This is no longer true. If the economy is to grow faster and unemployment is to be substantially reduced, the performance of the UK manufacturing sector is of vital importance. If manufacturing industry contracts, there is a real danger that the whole

The manufacturing myth

It is still common to refer to OECD members as the "industrialised economies". Common, yet quite wrong. Manufacturing firms now employ just one worker in six in America, one in five in Britain and one in three in Germany and Japan.

The decline of manufacturing in the past two decades has been steepest in Britain, where manufacturing employment has tumbled by almost half since 1970. In most other countries the fall has been slower. In the same period, America has shed 8% of its manufacturing jobs; France has lost 18%; and Germany has lost 17%. Japan, however, is a notable exception – it has added about 20% to manufacturing payrolls over the same period.

Services now account for more than half the output – and well over half the jobs – in OECD countries. The rich industrial economies might therefore be better dubbed the "service economies".

Does it matter that manufacturing provides fewer people with their livelihoods? Many believe that it does: they see it as both a cause and a symptom of more general economic decline.

The "manufacturing matters" school claims that manufacturing jobs are superior to service jobs in several ways. It is often argued that such work is tangible in a way that service jobs are not. Another popular view is that jobs in manufacturing demand more skills than those in services. The evidence, however, does not bear out these claims.

There is a more fundamental reason why the shift of employment from manufacturing to services is less worrying than some economists and politicians claim. Changes in manufacturing and service businesses have blurred the distinction between the two. So much so, indeed, that it may now be of little use. Manufacturers have come to rely on services for a greater proportion of their inputs. Cars, computers and hi-fis are not merely manufactured – they are also designed, marketed, advertised and distributed. A significant and rising part of the value added by manufacturers now consists of services.

The decline of manufacturing employment and the rise of service-sector jobs is also a consequence of changes in the way manufacturing companies are organised. Most manufacturing firms used to provide a wide range of services in-house. They employed their own accountants, cleaners and cooks. These days, however, they are more likely to buy in auditing, cleaning, catering and other business services from specialised service companies. *Some of the shift from manufacturing to service employment is therefore a statistical illusion.*

But to the extent that the decline in manufacturing employment is real, how should the governments of OECD countries respond? All of them are continually bombarded with demands to prevent further shrinkage of manufacturing through subsidies or trade protection. But subsidies and import tariffs would do nothing to encourage efficiency in manufacturing industries. Indeed, in the long run, they would do much harm: by diverting resources away from more productive sectors, they would hinder the creation of jobs elsewhere in the economy. The end result would be fewer overall jobs – in both manufacturing and services.

Abridged from *The Economist*, 19 March 1994

economy will stagnate through a lack of technological dynamism and severe balance of payments constraints on growth.

Unemployment

Deindustrialization will lead to **unemployment** if the growth of employment elsewhere in the economy is insufficient to absorb the labour shed by the manufacturing sector (unless the size of the workforce declines).

Since 1966, deindustrialization has contributed to higher unemployment in the UK – see Table 6, the figures in which are taken from various issues of the *Annual Abstract of Statistics*.

Table 6 Changes in employment, 1966–95 (thousands)

	1966–79*	1979–83†	1983–90†	1990–95‡
Change in labour force	+154	+241	+1826	−759
Change in total employment	−959	−2106	+1788	−1020
Change in unemployment	+1063	+1640	−1429	+699
Change in employment in:				
Agriculture	−110	−30	−51	+3
Manufacturing	−2008	−1728	−479	−785
Other production industries				
and construction	−706	−268	−196	−469
Services	+865	−81	+2328	+226
Change in self-employment				
and armed forces	+90	+343	+1058	−240

* Standard Industrial Classification (SIC) 1968; †SIC 1980; ‡SIC 1992

- Agriculture and production industries other than manufacturing (construction, mining and oil and gas production) shed over 0.8 million jobs between 1966 and 1979, while over 2 million jobs were lost in the manufacturing sector itself. The increase in jobs created by the service sector was insufficient to absorb the loss of jobs in manufacturing – so that, together with a very small increase in the size of the labour force, unemployment rose by over one million.
- Then, between 1979 and 1983, employment fell in all of the sectors listed; manufacturing in particular lost 1.7 million jobs while unemployment rose by a similar number.
- With the upturn in economic activity, employment rose from the trough in 1983 to the peak in 1990 by 1.8 million. However, all of the net creation of jobs was in services; the manufacturing sector

shed nearly half a million more jobs over the period. The labour force increased by 1.8 million, so that without a substantial increase in self-employment, unemployment would not have fallen by 1.4 million. Employment creation in the service sector alone, even during the upturn, was only just able to compensate for the continued fall in manufacturing employment and the increase in the size of the labour force.

- In 1990 the economy went into recession again – following the **overheating** of the economy due to a consumer-led boom in the late 1980s. Employment fell by over one million between 1990 and 1995, and unemployment rose again by 0.7 million to 2.3 million. Employment in manufacturing fell by 0.8 million, and in other production industries by nearly half a million. (The figures in the table for the period 1990–95 use the SIC 1992 classification, and the figures are somewhat different in size when compared with the previous SIC 1980 classification, which is only available up to 1994.)

In view of the failure of the economy to create a sufficient number of alternative jobs, it is clear that the ongoing decline in manufacturing employment, exacerbated by the recessions of the early 1980s and early 90s, has left a large **structural component** in unemployment. It is unlikely that unemployment can be brought down to levels which could be regarded as being compatible with 'full employment' without arresting the process of deindustrialization.

Growth

A related, though conceptually distinct, worry about deindustrialization concerns the role that the manufacturing sector plays in the process of **economic growth**. It is often asserted that the manufacturing sector is the 'engine of growth', for reasons summed up in what have become known as **Kaldor's Growth Laws**, named after the great Cambridge economist. There are three laws to consider.

- The first law states that there is a strong positive relationship between the growth of manufacturing industry and the growth rate of the economy as a whole in a causal sense – and not simply because manufacturing activity constitutes a large fraction of gross domestic product (GDP). The second and third laws are concerned with accounting for this strong positive relationship.
- The second law states that there is a strong positive relationship between the growth of manufacturing output and the rate of growth of productivity in manufacturing.
- The third law states that there is a strong positive relationship

between the rate at which manufacturing output and employment grows and the rate at which productivity grows outside manufacturing, because resources are used which otherwise would have been unemployed or have a lower productivity.

- **The first growth law**

Professor Kaldor, in his analysis of growth-rate differences between twelve OECD countries, found a strong correlation between the rate of growth of manufacturing output and the growth of GDP; and the faster the rate of growth of manufacturing relative to the growth of GDP, the faster the growth of national income. In other words, *what distinguishes fast-growing countries from slow-growing countries is whether the share of manufacturing in total output is increasing or not.*

Since growth-rate differences between countries are largely accounted for by differences in productivity growth (that is, differences in the growth of output per person), rather than differences in the rate of growth of the labour force, Kaldor concluded that there must be a relationship between the rate at which manufacturing output grows and the rate at which productivity grows inside and outside manufacturing. This was also confirmed by his research, and has been supported by other research. This leads to the second and third laws.

- **The second growth law**

As far as productivity growth in manufacturing is concerned, Kaldor found that, on average, a 1 per cent growth of output leads to a 0.5 per cent increase in productivity growth. This relationship – the second law – arises from the existence of *increasing returns to scale* in the manufacturing sector, both static and dynamic.

Static increasing returns to scale means that if all inputs are increased, output rises by more than in proportion to the increase in inputs, leading to an increase in output per person.

Dynamic increasing returns to scale are largely related to technical progress embodied in capital goods, which means that the faster the rate of capital accumulation associated with output growth, the faster the rate of growth of labour productivity. An increase in the rate of growth of output therefore leads to a cumulative expansion via increased productivity. These characteristics do not appear to be found in sectors other than manufacturing.

This second law is also sometimes known as Verdoorn's Law after the Dutch economist P.J. Verdoorn who first mooted the relationship.

- **The third growth law**

As far as productivity growth outside manufacturing is concerned, Kaldor found a strong *negative* relationship between productivity growth in the economy as a whole and employment growth outside manufacturing (for a given rate of growth of employment in manufacturing). This indicates that fast employment growth in non-manufacturing activities slows up overall productivity growth, and vice versa. This is because, very often, there is only a very loose relationship between output and employment in sectors like agriculture, retailing and other service activities, so that when employment rises or falls, output hardly changes at all. This phenomenon is often referred to as **disguised unemployment**.

Disguised unemployment is very prevalent in the agricultural sector of Third World countries and in the petty service trades found in urban areas; but it is a phenomenon also found in more industrialized countries. Many activities outside manufacturing are also subject to **diminishing returns**, so that if the labour force is reduced, the marginal product of labour, and the overall level of productivity, rises.

- **The cumulative effect**

Taken together, these three main growth 'laws' mean that a country which obtains an initial advantage in productive activities that have favourable growth characteristics will tend to sustain that advantage by exploiting increasing returns to scale, both static and dynamic, leading to higher productivity and improved competitiveness.

For example, a favourable shock that increases the rate of growth of output in manufacturing will lead to faster productivity growth, which in turn, by making goods more competitive, expands the demand for output, which again induces productivity growth, and so on. This is sometimes called a **virtuous circle of growth**. If, as we observed since 1966, the rate of growth of manufacturing has been stagnant or it declines, the opposite occurs, creating a **vicious circle** of low economic growth, low productivity growth, deteriorating competitiveness and the shedding of labour from the manufacturing sector owing to lack of domestic and foreign demand for the products.

The balance of payments

While the foregoing laws can explain differences in the growth experience of countries, the initial impetus to the growth of manufacturing output is not determined. Historically, the stimulus has come from the agricultural sector in the early stages of development and from exports in the later stages.

One of the major reasons why the UK was the first country to industrialize was that it experienced an early agricultural revolution which raised productivity in agriculture and increased the demand for manufactured goods, both as inputs and as finished products. But the UK did not choose to specialize in agriculture, nor is it rich in raw materials. The lack of self-sufficiency in food and the paucity of raw materials leads us on to the third reason why manufacturing matters, namely the **balance of payments.**

The UK needs to import foodstuffs and raw materials, and to pay for these – in order to maintain equilibrium on the balance of payments current account – the UK exports mainly manufactured goods, various services ('invisibles'), and more recently North Sea oil. North Sea oil production has already begun to level off and will generate lower export earnings in the future, unless the dollar price of oil rises by more than in proportion to the fall in output. This will increasingly leave exports of services and manufactured goods to pay for the necessary imports of food and raw materials (including oil in the future).

Traditionally, the balance of trade in goods – the **visible balance** – has been in deficit, although exports of manufactured goods used to exceed imports of manufactures. The latter is now no longer true. Since 1983 the balance of trade in manufactured goods has been in deficit, and the trend appears to be deteriorating. This means that only a surplus of trade in services – the **invisible balance** – is left to pay for food, raw material requirements and the appetite for foreign manufactured goods. *This is not a sustainable situation, and without any improvement in the manufacturing trade balance, the growth of the whole economy will have to be slowed up to cut back imports.*

This leads to the important concept of **balance of payments constrained growth,** and the measurement of a country's balance of payments equilibrium growth rate.

- **Balance of payments equilibrium growth rate**

For the current account of the balance of payments to balance, the value of exported goods and services must equal the value of imported goods and services. For an equilibrium to be preserved, the rates of growth of the values of exports and imports must be equal.

How fast the value of exports grows depends firstly on how fast export prices are growing; and secondly on how fast the demand for exports is growing. The rate of growth of the demand for exports in turn will depend partly on price competitiveness and partly on how fast world trade, or income, is growing. Likewise for imports, except that it is the growth of domestic income (or more accurately, expenditure) rather than world trade that counts.

• Elasticity

The relationship between the growth of exports (or imports) and relative price changes is called the **price elasticity of demand** for exports (or imports). The relationship between the growth of demand for imports (or exports) and the growth of domestic (or world) income is called the **income elasticity of demand** for imports (or exports).

If we make the assumption that in the long run there is very little change in the relative prices of exports and imports, measured in a common currency, then the growth of imports and exports is dominated by income changes at home and abroad. There will exist a rate of growth of domestic income which just keeps the growth of imports in line with the growth of exports. That growth of income which is consistent with balance of payments equilibrium on current account defines a country's balance of payments **equilibrium growth rate**. This rate is equal to the growth of world income multiplied by the ratio of the income elasticity of demand for UK exports to the income elasticity of demand for imports in the UK. This can be measured approximately as the ratio of the rate of growth of exports to the income elasticity of demand for imports. This is illustrated in Figure 4.

X_1 and X_2 show different levels of *export growth*. Lines $0M_1$ and $0M_2$ show the relationships between import growth and GDP growth, so that the slopes of the curves measure the *income elasticity of demand for imports*. The steeper the curve the higher the income

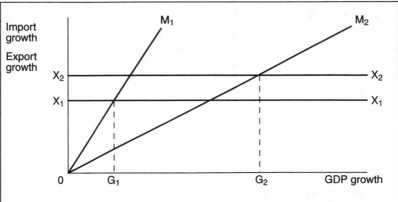

Figure 4 A country's balance of payments constrained growth rate

elasticity. Where the X and M lines cross determines the GDP growth rate consistent with balance of payments equilibrium.

It can immediately be seen that a country with a low export growth (X_1) and a high income elasticity of demand for imports (M_1) will have a lower growth rate (G_1) than a country with a high rate of growth of exports (X_2) and a lower income elasticity of demand for imports (M_2), whose growth rate will be G_2.

This equilibrium growth rate determines the rate of economic growth that a country can sustain without encountering balance of payments difficulties – the balance of payments constrained growth rate. No country can grow faster for very long than the rate of growth consistent with balance of payments equilibrium on the current account, because there is a limit to the ability and willingness to finance deficits.

There is a very close correlation between balance of payments equilibrium growth rates and the actual growth rates experienced by advanced industrialized countries over long periods. In particular, through the period of the 1950s to the 1970s the UK had the lowest equilibrium and actual growth rates of all the major industrialized countries, with Japan, Germany, Italy and France having the highest actual and equilibrium rates. *Successful countries are those that have high elasticities for their exports with respect to world income and low income elasticities of demand for imports.*

In fact, for the UK, the latter elasticity is not particularly high compared with other advanced industrialized countries. The low balance of payments equilibrium growth rate – and therefore the low actual growth rate – in the UK is due primarily to a low world income elasticity for UK exports (hardly greater than unity compared with a value of 3 for Japan). When foreigners' incomes rise, they tend to buy relatively few UK produced goods and services.

From the point of view of economic policy in the UK, any programme that aims to increase economic growth, other than one based on expanding exports, will soon run into a balance of payments constraint. A current account deficit will emerge and require offsetting capital flows from abroad or running down foreign exchange reserves. In order to attract foreign capital flows interest rates may have to be fixed higher than they otherwise would be, thus reducing investment, and the exchange rate would have to be protected from depreciating. If foreigners withdraw their capital owing to lack of confidence, or if they fear a depreciation of the currency, a sterling crisis will ensue and deflationary policies (to reduce import demand) will be required. *It is in this sense that the balance of payments equilibrium growth rate represents a constraint on economic growth.*

If the UK economy is going to experience sustainable job-creating growth, either exports must grow more rapidly or measures must be implemented to reduce the income elasticity of demand for imports. We return to these issues in Chapter 6.

Trade in services

The notion of a balance of payments equilibrium growth rate presented above concerns the whole of the current account of the balance of payments. By implication, a higher rate of growth consistent with current account equilibrium could be achieved by expanding exports of services and not just manufactured goods. However, there are three important reasons why exports of services are likely to be limited in ways that exports of manufactured goods are not.

- Trade in services is limited in the sense that only a small proportion of service output is tradeable (perhaps 20 per cent). Many services are produced or provided on the spot and cannot be packed up and sold abroad. According to the Input–Output table for the UK in 1990, the manufacturing sector exported 31 per cent of its value-added while the service sector exported less than 8 per cent. Financial and business services exported less than 7 per cent.

However, *The Economist* continues to strike a sceptical note in 'Making it' (see page 38) with its mystified: 'Why British politicians so love manufacturing is hard to explain…'.

- The sheer magnitude of manufactured exports dwarfs exports of services. In 1993, the value of exports of manufactured goods amounted to £100 billion while services represented only £33 billion.
- In both services and manufacturing, the UK's share of world exports has fallen. Between 1968 and 1992 the share of manufactured exports fell from 9.6 to 7.2 per cent while the share of exports of services fell more noticeably from 11.9 to 8.4 per cent.

While it is clear that services make an important contribution to the current account, it is unlikely that the growth of exports necessary to raise the rate of growth of the economy consistent with balance of payments equilibrium can be provided by the service sector. Exports of manufactured goods are far more important in terms of their contribution to the value of total UK exports and in terms of growth, both actual and potential. This contribution will become increasingly important as earnings from oil exports decline over the next 20 years, and as international trade in services becomes more intense.

Making it

"I DO not believe it is possible for Britain to trade its way into the future primarily as a service-dominated economy… A robust manufacturing base is a crucial element in a modern competitive economy." Thus, Tony Blair, the Labour leader, on 11 June, stating what is now conventional wisdom among British politicians after a brief period during the 1980s when the Tories bravely rose above it. Yet, whatever a future Labour government might do to boost manufacturing (and judging from Mr Blair's speech, it will not be much), manufacturing's share of Britain's GDP is likely to fall steadily, as it has since 1960. The fact is that Britain, contrary to Mr Blair's belief, already has a service-dominated economy.

Why British politicians so love manufacturing is hard to explain. Perhaps they recall that, when Britain was primarily a maker of things, it was also a global power. Kenneth Clarke, the chancellor, shares the obsession. He justified last week's interest-rate cut by pointing to the lacklustre performance of manufacturing – output fell by 0.3% between March and April, and was barely up on a year earlier. He played down evidence of rising consumer confidence and spending, much of it in the service sector, which dwarfs manufacturing. Unemployment fell by 14,800 in May, to its lowest for five years, suggesting that the economy had no need of a rate cut.

Manufacturing dominates the political debate about Britain's economic performance. Mr Blair, for instance, accused British manufacturers of under-investing. Michael Heseltine, the deputy prime minister, countered by publishing a paper, "The UK's investment performance: fact and fallacy". This claimed that British manufacturers' ratio of investment to output matched that of German and American firms, and disputed the view that British manufacturing plant and machinery is older than that of other industrial countries.

Mr Blair quoted, approvingly, Adair Turner, the director-general of the Confederation of British Industry: "Despite the vitally important relative improvements in manufacturing over the last 12 to 15 years, UK productivity is still lagging behind major competitors." He took this to mean that the CBI thinks Britain is only halfway through a manufacturing recovery, and still has far to go.

But Mr Blair missed the main point of the speech by Mr Turner from which the quote was lifted, which is that manufacturing is unlikely to be the main source of economic gains in the future. The big opportunity, and challenge for government, lies in improving the efficiency of the non-traded sectors of the economy, many of which are services. Mr Turner thinks Britain has done well in these sectors of late – compared with continental Europe, if not America – but that much remains undone. Some fresh thinking on this from Labour and the Tories, and less nostalgia for Britain's manufacturing past, would be welcome.

The Economist, 15 June 1996

Conclusion

As a conclusion to this chapter we can do no better than reproduce selected quotations from the Report of the House of Lords Select Committee on Science and Technology in 1991:

- 'We must have a concerted campaign to promote greater esteem for manufacturing industry.'
- 'Government must lead this campaign and proclaim the central position of manufacturing to our national prosperity.'
- 'All the evidence shows that the present lack of government commitment, support and assistance is deeply damaging to industry and to our national interest.'
- 'Only a substantial increase in manufacturing output can correct the huge deficit on our balance of trade.'
- 'Action is needed now to stop the decline of our manufacturing industry.'
- 'The most urgent need is for a change in our culture. Unless we revise radically some of the attitudes which permeate our society we will continue to be neglected. Antipathy to manufacturing industry runs deep in our society.'

KEY WORDS

Unemployment
Overheating
Structural component
Economic growth
Kaldor's Growth Laws
Static/dynamic increasing
   returns to scale
Disguised unemployment
Diminishing returns

Virtuous circle of growth
Vicious circle
Balance of payments
Visible/invisible balances
Price/income elasticities
   of demand
Equilibrium growth rate
Constrained growth rate

Reading list

Healey, N. and Cook, M., Chapter 2 in *Supply Side Economics,* 3rd edn, Heinemann Educational, 1996.

Essay topics

1. Explain what is meant by the balance of payments and whether or not a deficit on the visible balance should be regarded as a problem by the government. Discuss the factors responsible for the UK's

trade record in recent years and evaluate their importance for the future economic performance of the country. [25 marks]
[Northern Examinations and Assessment Board 1993]
2. (a) To what extent should a country be concerned about a persistent balance of payments deficit on current account? [40 marks]
(b) Evaluate the measures which the UK government could use *in the 1990s* to reduce such a deficit. [60 marks]
[University of London Examinations and Assessment Council 1996]
3. 'When the manufacturing sector is unable to export enough to pay for the full employment level of imports deindustrialization has begun.' (Ajit Singh)
(a) Is the statement an adequate definition of deindustrialization? [10 marks]
(b) Does deindustrialization really matter? Explain your answer. [10 marks]
[University of Cambridge Local Examinations Syndicate 1996]

Data Response Question

This task is based on a question set by the University of Cambridge Local Examinations Syndicate in 1996. Read the piece below and study Table A (adapted from *The Economist*, 6–12 August 1994). Then answer the questions.

The balance of trade: a constraint on growth?

It has been argued that one of the reasons for the UK's relatively poor economic performance over the past 50 years has been the constraint on economic growth caused by repeated problems with the balance of payments, and the consequent actions which governments have taken.

Often, when faced with balance of payments difficulties, the government has followed a deflationary macroeconomic policy; this has had the effect of reducing the level of economic activity, and so restricting growth in output and living standards.

Increases in national output, however, result from the interplay of many factors, and sometimes occur at the same time as balance of payments problems. Table A shows some relevant aspects of the economies of the UK and five other nations in the early 1990s.

Table A

Country	Balance of visible trade	Balance of payments on current account	Exchange rate (trade-weighted index, 1985 = 100)		1995 forecasts		
	(1993 $ billion)	(1993 $ billion)	1993	1994	Balance of payments on current account (% of GDP)	% change in retail prices	% change in real GDP
UK	−19	−12	82	79	−2.1	3.7	3.2
France	+16	+13	105	110	0.6	1.8	2.9
Germany	+43	−22	123	126	−0.6	2.2	2.1
Italy	+19	+8	80	76	1.5	3.5	2.5
Japan	+143	+132	187	189	2.2	0.7	2.1
USA	−147	−116	66	64	−1.9	3.5	3.0

Source: Adapted from *The Economist,* 6–12 August 1994

1. (a) How is the balance of visible trade calculated? [2 marks]
   (b) Which country had the largest deficit in its invisible trade in 1993? Give a reason that might explain this. [2 marks]
   (c) Compare the current account balance of payments of the UK in 1993 with that of Italy. [3 marks]
2. Economic theory suggests that under certain conditions a country experiencing a current account deficit (or surplus) is likely to see a fall (or rise) in the foreign exchange value of its currency. Identify which two countries in the table do *not* show such a relationship, and explain *one* reason for this. [4 marks]
3. (a) Compare the forecast performance of the UK economy in 1995 with that of the other five countries shown in the table. [3 marks]
   (b) The information in the table suggests that the UK's overseas trade performance was not on its own expected to be a major constraint on the forecast growth rate. Suggest why balance of payments problems might be thought likely to act as such a constraint, and discuss why they may not do so in practice. [6 marks]

Chapter Four

The causes of deindustrialization since 1966

'When the manufacturing sector is unable to export enough to pay for the full employment level of imports deindustrialization has begun.'
Ajit Singh

Five main views have been put forward to explain the process of deindustrialization:

- technical progress;
- the Bacon and Eltis thesis;
- under-investment in UK manufacturing industry;
- the impact of North Sea oil; and
- the weak trade performance of the UK manufacturing sector.

Each of these purports to explain the long-term decline in manufacturing employment. In assessing these isssues, we shall also look at wider evidence to check their consistency.

Technical progress

It is claimed that technical progress has led to capital displacing labour in the production process. We know from the concept of the **production function**, which relates output to inputs, that labour and capital are used together to produce output. In explaining deindustrialization, it is claimed that technical progress has been of a labour-saving nature.

Figure 5 plots trends for the capital stock, employment and output in manufacturing for the period 1966–94. It is clear that the capital stock has grown fairly smoothly while the trend in employment is downwards, although with cyclical variations. Manufacturing output also follows a cyclical pattern: growing up to 1973, then falling to a low in the slump of 1979–82; rising to a new peak in 1989 and declining until 1992 before taking off again.

Since the capital stock is fixed in the short run, it is employment that adjusts to cyclical fluctuations in output. However, it is not possible to conclude that technical progress was labour-saving merely because the capital stock was growing while employment in manufacturing was falling secularly. As the price of labour rises relative to

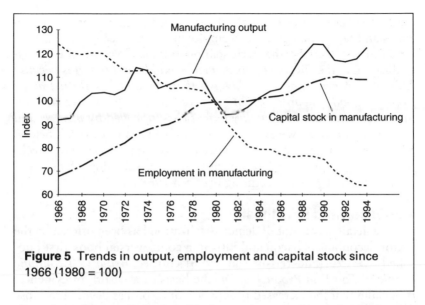

Figure 5 Trends in output, employment and capital stock since 1966 (1980 = 100)

the price of capital, there will always be a process of substitution going on. Having said this, it is almost certainly the case that in certain industries within manufacturing, increased mechanization resulting from technical progress will have displaced labour.

But one must distinguish clearly the microeconomic consequences of technical progress from the macroeconomic consequences. There is no reason why, at the aggregate level, technical progress should mean less manufacturing employment. Technical progress involves **process innovation** or **product innovation** or both:

- *Process innovation* at a given level of output, involving capital in new ways of producing things, will lead to the displacement of labour, but at the same time will involve more investment which increases aggregate demand, and therefore employment.
- *Product innovation* at a given level of output may or may not displace labour. New products and more competitive products increase demand, and therefore can create more employment.

Examples of employment-creating product innovations are the washing machine, motor vehicle and aeroplane; while the microchip, which has permitted increased mechanization, has also created microcomputers and pocket calculators and has improved the quality and sophistication of existing products over a wide spectrum.

Historically, technical progress has created more jobs than it has destroyed at the aggregate level. Furthermore, it is important to point out that in the most technologically advanced countries of the United States and Japan, manufacturing employment has been growing.

Contrary to the view that technical progress is the cause of deindustrialization in the UK, *the opposite view could be put that it is because technical progress has been sluggish that demand has shifted away from UK goods towards foreign-produced goods whose price competitiveness, reliability and quality have been improved by process and product innovation.* We examine this possibility in more detail below. While no quantitative conclusions are possible, it is our view that technical progress cannot be responsible for the shedding of nearly 5 million jobs in UK manufacturing between 1966 and 1994.

The Bacon and Eltis thesis

A more detailed account of deindustrialization has been offered by the Oxford economists Bacon and Eltis in a controversial book first published in 1976 (and reissued in 1996) entitled *Britain's Economic Problem: Too Few Producers.* On the basis of a wealth of evidence, they claim that the increased proportion of resources devoted to those public sector activities that do not market their output (including the old loss-making nationalized industries) has **crowded out** resources available to the manufacturing sector and other sectors that do market their output.

Bacon and Eltis point out that exports and imports are made up solely of **marketable output,** while consumption and investment may either be marketable or **non-marketable output.** They claim that employment outside the marketable output sector rose by roughly one-third relative to employment in the marketable output sector from 1961 to 1974, apparently far in excess of other countries. Employment in education increased by 76 per cent, local government employment increased by 54 per cent, and central government employment by 10 per cent (all producing non-marketable output). Wages in these occupations also rose in excess of the average, and the effect on the economy as a whole was a fall in profits net of tax to the detriment of investment in the marketable output sector.

Had the industrial base been strengthened by more investment in the marketable output sector, deindustrialization would have been considerably reduced and the overall macroeconomic performance of the economy would have been much healthier.

- **Weaknesses in the Bacon–Eltis argument**

There are several weaknesses in the argument. The essential task is to show that non-market activities have starved the manufacturing sector of resources – especially labour and investment funds – which would otherwise have been productively used in manufacturing.

* On the labour shortage hypothesis, the Bacon and Eltis argument is not supported by the facts. Between 1966 and 1976, the labour shed by the manufacturing sector was mainly male whereas the labour employed in the public sector was mainly female. The manufacturing sector was not starved of labour by the growth of employment in the public sector. Furthermore, since the early 1980s there has been a permanent pool of unemployed labour.

* As far as investment is concerned, it is possible that the resources required by a growing public sector could have reduced the funds available for profitable investment in the market sector. With labour productivity growing faster than the demand for output, labour will be shed from manufacturing unless there is investment in new and technologically advanced activities. Was there crowding out of investment from the private sector?

The proportion of private sector investment in total investment was at its lowest (53 per cent) in 1967. Since then it rose to 71 per cent in 1979 and reached a peak of 86 per cent in 1989 before falling back again. If the Bacon and Eltis thesis were correct we would expect a gradual but constant downward trend in the proportion of investment stemming from the private sector. Apart from the period before 1967, this does not appear to be the case.

In the light of the evidence, it is hard to sustain the view that the growth of the non-market sector has been a cause of deindustrialization. Furthermore, the reform of the public sector and the privatization of many of the old nationalized industries in the 1980s have not had any significant effect on revitalizing the growth of the manufacturing sector.

Under-investment in UK manufacturing industry

Even though it is hard to sustain the view that the growth of the public sector has starved the private sector of resources, there is a general consensus that there has been too little investment in British manufacturing industry since the Second World War, and particularly since the 1960s, which has eroded Britain's **competitiveness** and been a major cause of deindustrialization.

There is some force in this argument, which links up with our preferred explanation which is based on the UK's weak trade performance (see below). The UK has one of the lowest ratios of investment to GDP of any advanced industrial nation, which affects

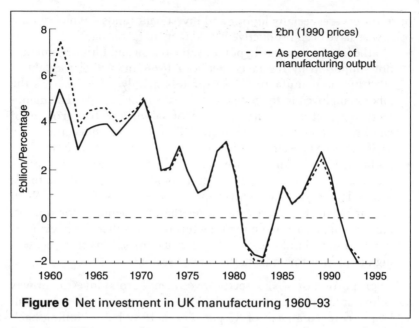

Figure 6 Net investment in UK manufacturing 1960–93

both the ability to produce and competitiveness to the extent that technical progress is embodied in investment. Moreover, as Figure 6 shows, the level of real manufacturing investment has been on a downward trend since 1960.

There are many economic and institutional explanations that can be mentioned for the UK's poor investment record, such as:

- an anti-industrial culture;
- a risky, fluctuating macroeconomic environment;
- low research and development expenditure;
- the dominance of the City of London and the cult of short-termism – the desire for a quick profit.

As Michael Heseltine, then President of the Board of Trade, admitted in the House of Commons in 1993:

> I do not doubt for one moment that deep-seated short-term attitudes ... is one important strand in understanding why we as a nation have performed less well than many of our competitors. Such attitudes have led us to invest less than we might in technology and advanced means of production.

North Sea oil and the 'Dutch disease'

Another explanation of the more recent demise of manufacturing industry concerns the discovery and export of **North Sea oil**.

Naked truth on investment

From Prof. M.P. Taylor

Sir, I was shocked to read ("Heseltine poised to defend UK's investment record", 4 March) that the deputy prime minister's argument that Britain's investment needs are less than hitherto is supported by the Economics Department at Liverpool University.

The UK's chronic problem is poor international competitiveness. This is due to low productivity which, in turn, follows from low investment.

As a proportion of gross domestic product invested over the period since 1979, the UK lags behind the other G7 countries, behind other European ones and all 24 other OECD countries. This is the main reason why the UK's trade in manufactured goods went into deficit in 1983 for the first time since the industrial revolution and has remained there. This is why the UK's visible trade deficit with the rest of the EU is second only to that of Greece.

It is ridiculous to argue that adopting Japanese production or management techniques results in less need for investment when the UK's investment rate is roughly half that of Japan.

Another way of seeing the link between investment and productivity is to compare British and foreign owned companies in the UK.

Foreign owned companies account for 17.2 per cent of private employment but produce 21.7 per cent of all value-added in the UK economy.

British owned companies account for 82.8 per cent of employment and 78.3 per cent of value added. Foreign owned companies are thus 34 per cent more productive in value added per employee. But foreign owned companies re-invest 19 per cent of value added compared to 10 per cent by British owned companies.

While my colleague, Prof. Patrick Minford, may wish to support Mr Heseltine's politically sophisticated but economically naive arguments, there are many of us in the economics profession who refuse to see the emperor's clothes when it is clear that he isn't wearing any.

Mark P. Taylor
University of Liverpool

Financial Times, 15 March 1996

- **The theory**

The discovery and export of a natural resource increases the supply of foreign exchange to a country. If the assumption is made that import demand remains the same (e.g. because of full employment), the exchange rate will appreciate because the exchange rate is determined by the supply and demand for foreign currency. If oil is priced in dollars, for example, and there is an increase in the supply of dollars, the sterling price of dollars will fall, or the dollar price of sterling rises (i.e. sterling appreciates in value). This then reduces the demand for other tradeable goods, and contracts output. This is the so-called **'Dutch disease'**, following the experience of the Netherlands after the discovery of natural gas in the 1960s.

- **The facts**

On the surface this explanation of deindustrialization would seem to fit the facts of the late 1970s when oil production increased rapidly along with exports of fuels. The extraction of North Sea oil began in earnest in 1976 and grew rapidly thereafter. By 1983 the volume of fuel exports was four times higher than in 1975. However, the effective exchange rate – the exchange rate relative to a basket of currencies – did not begin to appreciate until 1978, when fuel exports rose by 43 per cent in one year, suggesting that the impact of oil on the manufacturing sector could not have occurred until the very late 1970s.

Furthermore, there is nothing inevitable about currency appreciation following a natural-resource discovery which earns foreign exchange. There are many ways in which additional foreign exchange can be used, especially if the economy is not at full employment. How the exchange rate moves is at the discretion of the monetary authorities. The fact the exchange rate was allowed to rise after 1978 undoubtedly contributed to the contraction of manufacturing industry; *but it was not the inevitable result of North Sea oil.* In any case, the process of deindustrialization began in the 1960s, and as a long-term trend it has nothing to do with the relatively recent exploitation of North Sea oil.

If we consider long-run trends, a more convincing explanation lies in the weak trade performance of the UK manufacturing sector, particularly the slow growth of exports relative to the propensity to import, as outlined in the previous chapter.

Weak trade performance

The importance of manufacturing industry for the UK balance of payments has already been emphasized above. The **balance of trade** in manufactured goods has traditionally been in surplus, but the surplus has gradually dwindled since the mid-1960s, as shown by Figure 7.

In 1965, the value of exports of manufactured goods was more than 180 per cent of the value of imports, and by 1974 it had fallen to less than 120 per cent. Since then the trend has continued downwards with fluctuations towards the point where, in 1983, there was for the first time in history a deficit on the balance of trade in manufactured goods.

It is the weak trade performance of the manufacturing sector, reflected in the gradual elimination of the trade surplus, that provides the most convincing explanation of deindustrialization – as measured by the absolute long-term decline in employment in the manufacturing sector. The fact is that UK manufacturers have not been able to sell enough, either at home or abroad, for the growth of output in manufacturing to exceed the growth of labour productivity, and inevitably

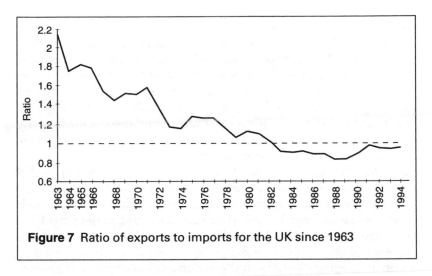

Figure 7 Ratio of exports to imports for the UK since 1963

employment has decreased as explained in Chapter 2. Exports have not grown fast enough, and imported manufactured goods have steadily penetrated the UK market, as shown by the trends in Table 7.

This fits in with the analysis of Dr Singh of Cambridge University who argues that 'deindustrialization occurs when the manufacturing sector, without losing price or cost competitiveness, is unable to pay for the full employment level of imports'.

Table 7 shows how **import penetration** – which reduces the growth of UK manufacturers' sales in the UK – has risen since 1968. In aggregate, foreign producers increased their share of the UK market for manufactured goods from 17 per cent in 1968 to 43 per cent in 1994, an increase of more than 150 per cent. Sectors experiencing the

Table 7 Import penetration and exports as a proportion of manufacturers' sales

	Imports as a percentage of home demand	Exports as a percentage of manufacturers' sales
1968	17	17
1974	23.3	21.3
1979	25.8	24.3
1983	31.1	26.6
1989	36.7	30
1994*	43	39

* The 1994 figure is calculated on a different definition of manufactured products from the previous years

greatest import penetration were chemicals and artificial fibres, electrical and electronic engineering, motor vehicles, textiles, and leather goods.

On the other hand, exports have grown more slowly as a proportion of manufacturers' sales, rising from 17 per cent to 30 per cent between 1968 and 1989. Even this increase is deceptive since increased import penetration has reduced the growth of home sales (and therefore the growth of total sales) of UK manufacturers, thus introducing bias into export performance when it is measured by the share of exports in total sales – the **exports-to-sales ratio**.

Overall, there can be no doubt that the trade performance of the UK manufacturing sector has worsened since 1968, and this is reflected in growing import penetration and the gradual elimination of the trade surplus since the mid-1960s, while manufacturing employment has fallen and unemployment has grown.

- **An increasing deficit with the European Union**
A further dimension of the problem is revealed in Table 8, which shows the balance of trade in manufactured goods with various blocs of countries.

The most noticeable feature in the pattern of trade is the increasing deficit with countries in the European Union since 1973, the year in which the UK joined.
- In 1970, the UK had a trade surplus in manufactured goods with each bloc listed in Table 8, except North America.
- By 1974, the UK had a trade deficit with each bloc except for 'other countries'.

Table 8 UK balance of trade in manufactures with other blocs of countries, 1970–93 (£million)

	European Community/ Union	Other West European countries	North America	Other countries
1970	+164	+457	−210	+1861
1974	−646	−50	−222	+2675
1978	−1615	−784	−147	+6464
1982	−4983	−1028	−1362	+7574
1987	−11085	−2796	−1398	+5333
1990	−9929	−3191	−2050	+1258
1993	−2987	−2692	−1751	−1728

Source: Overseas trade statistics, various years

- Throughout the 1980s the situation continued to worsen, but more so with the EU than elsewhere.
- At the beginning of the 1990s the deficit with the EU fell substantially, owing mainly to the severe recession in the UK and partly to the depreciation of sterling after its exit from the European Exchange Rate Mechanism (ERM) in 1992.

Why is the UK weak in manufacturing?

In Chapter 3 it was noted that demand depends on relative prices and income. A low demand for UK-produced goods may result, therefore, from a high relative price via the price elasticity of demand and/or a low income elasticity of demand in the presence of rising real income. The cause of the problem can therefore be analysed in terms, on the one hand, of **price competitiveness** and, on the other hand, of the **non-price factors** which make UK goods less desirable to consumers when their income rises.

- ### Relative unit labour costs

Much emphasis is often placed on a lack of price competitiveness as the reason for the poor trade performance of the UK manufacturing sector. This assertion is usually supported by a list of factors that have contributed to increased costs – such as trade union militancy, low productivity, inefficient management, low investment, high exchange rates and uncoordinated industrial policy.

Each of these factors can contribute to a lack of competitiveness, but it is first necessary to show that over a long period there has been a progressive erosion of cost competitiveness, and therefore price competitiveness. We need to look at the costs or prices of UK manufactured goods relative to those of other countries – with adjustment for exchange rate changes.

A common measure of competitiveness is the **IMF index of relative unit labour costs**, which is shown in Figure 8 for the period 1963–94. **Relative producer prices** are also shown; these incorporate costs other than labour costs and are likely to give a more representative index of competitiveness. An increase in either index represents a reduction in competitiveness as the cost of UK goods rises relative to the cost of foreign goods.

- In fact, between 1963 and 1976, the indices moved in parallel on a downward trend. The competitiveness of UK products was *improving*, though not continuously.
- Following the effects of the 1967 devaluation of sterling, between

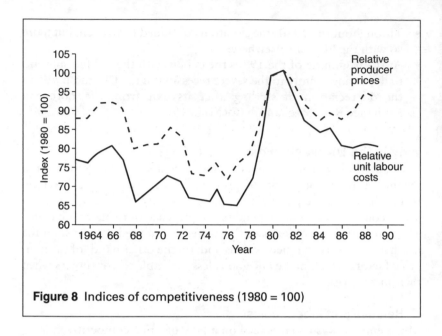

Figure 8 Indices of competitiveness (1980 = 100)

1968 and 1971 the indices both rose but not back to their original levels. However, by 1976 both indices indicate that competitiveness had improved by over 20 per cent from 1966.
- From 1976 to 1981, competitiveness deteriorated dramatically as a result of rapid wage inflation and later currency appreciation.
- After the early 1980s, competitiveness improved and was no worse in 1987 than in the middle of the 1960s.

Thus, as an overall explanation of the deterioration in the trade surplus in manufactured goods, the cost competitiveness argument is difficult to sustain.

- **Income elasticity of demand**
In any case, cost or price competitiveness is not the only determinant of the demand for goods. What is happening to income, and the characteristics of goods, are also extremely important.

If income increases, demand will increase if the product in question is a 'normal' good. According to the concept of the **income elasticity of demand**, we can distinguish between 'necessities', where the income elasticity is less than one (so that a 1 per cent increase in income is associated with an increase in demand of less than 1 per cent), and 'luxuries', where the income elasticity of demand is greater than one. A declining trade surplus in manufactured goods with improved competitiveness could occur if the goods produced by UK manufacturers in general possess a low income elasticity of demand, while those produced by competitors have a higher income elasticity.

Given that the balance of trade in manufactured goods has not moved in the expected direction when competitiveness improved means that increases in income in the UK and abroad, combined with differences in the income elasticity of demand, must have had the most important impact. *It is to the factors that make the income elasticity of demand for UK exports of manufactured goods low, and the income elasticity of demand for imports high, that we must look for the explanation of Britain's deteriorating trade performance in manufacturing.*

- ● **Non-price factors**

Research undertaken by the (now disbanded) National Economic Development Office (NEDO) points to the importance of non-price factors which have rendered UK manufactured goods in general relatively less desirable. Non-price competitiveness, which affects the income elasticity of demand, concerns factors such as:

- ● product quality and reliability
- ● design
- ● standard of after-sales service
- ● delivery.

The important determinants of non-price competitiveness are therefore expenditure on **research and development** (R&D), investment, and the way in which products are marketed.

Yet to gauge the actual degree of non-price competitiveness is difficult. How, for example, is the quality of a product measured? One approach is to argue that a purchaser chooses between goods on the basis of value for money and not simply on the basis of relative prices. If products are homogeneous there should, in the long term, be no differences in price and so prices diverge for reasons of product heterogeneity. If this is so, then it would be expected that products of better quality or which are technologically superior would have a higher value per tonne.

On this basis, work carried out by NEDO shows that in 1975 West German manufacturers were earning around 60 per cent more per tonne from exports of mechanical engineering products than were British manufacturers, and this is attributed to non-price factors.

- ● **Investment in manufacturing**

Investment is one of the key variables determining both price and non-price competitiveness. Investment enables productivity to increase, thus reducing unit costs, and enables the development and production of new products.

In real terms, investment in UK manufacturing was very sluggish through the 1960s and 70s, and increased by only 7 per cent in the period 1961–79 (peak to peak). As a proportion of value-added, it has varied cyclically around a ratio of 13 per cent. However, these figures include capital consumption; that is, investment expenditures undertaken to replace or maintain the existing capital stock. In *net terms*, the capital stock in manufacturing hardly grew at all, and the same has been true since 1979 (see Figure 6).

The Oxford economist, Walter Eltis, points out that investment in UK manufacturing has been mainly of the 'defensive' variety – constituting additions to the *existing* structure of the capital stock. Competitors, on the other hand, have devoted more expenditure to new machinery, new technology and new products. This is termed **'enterprise investment'**. Eltis attributes the lack of enterprise investment in UK manufacturing to:

- the low rate of return on capital in the sector relative to other sectors;
- the higher risk associated with investment in manufacturing because of its sensitivity to macroeconomic developments.

- ### Research and development (R&D)

A key element of investment is expenditure on R&D, which in turn leads to investment in new technology.

In the period 1971 to 1994, the UK spent around 2 per cent of its GNP on R&D. A quarter of this was in the defence sector, so that around 1.5 per cent was spent in normal commercial activities and this proportion hardly changed during the period. This compares with higher levels of non-defence R&D spending in Japan and Germany of more than 2.5 per cent in 1994, and about 2 per cent in the United States and France. Furthermore, R&D spending has risen as a proportion of GNP over the period in each of these countries and has been more or less constant in the UK.

- ### Attitudes towards manufacturing

Finally, it can be said that exporting has not been given sufficiently high priority at the national level, or by manufacturers themselves.

At the national level, as pointed out in a report of the House of Lords Select Committee on Overseas Trade, the most successful economies are those where exporting, and a thriving manufacturing industry in general, are regarded as the keys to economic success, and where the various actors – government, employers, trade unions and the financial

Incredible shrinking Britain

MICHAEL KITSON AND
JONATHAN MICHIE

Our research reveals manufacturing investment in Britain in the 1980s did little more than tread water. New investment was barely enough to maintain the 'capital stock' – the manufacturing infrastructure – let alone expand it, as our competitor countries have done.

As a result, by the end of the decade, German or American workers had, on average, 60 per cent more plant and equipment to work with than British workers. Our calculations show that investment by manufacturing firms (net of depreciation) – £3.5 billion a year on average in 1964–1973 and £2.2bn a year between 1973 and 1979 – plummeted to a mere £694m between 1979 and 1989.

However hard the remaining employees worked they could not compensate for the dramatic shrinking of the UK's industrial base. This is a very different picture from the one painted by the government, with its repeated claims that productivity rose during the 1980s. Output per worker did increase, but primarily because there were fewer workers, rather than because Britain was producing more goods.

Three million jobs have been lost in manufacturing in this country since 1979 – manufacturing employment has shrunk from more than 7 million to barely 4 million – a much bigger drop than in other industrialised countries.

Much of what little investment there was in industry was spent on cost cutting and downsizing rather than in greenfield sites or on developing new products. Thus, while for the vast majority of Organisation of Economic Cooperation and Development countries the growth rates of total and industrial research and development were much higher in the 1980s than in the 1970s – total expenditure rose from 1.4 per cent to 4.4 per cent in the US – the UK was a notable exception: here, R&D growth fell from 2.9 per cent to 2 per cent.

During the 1980s the UK was ranked 19th out of 22 OECD countries in manufacturing growth rate. Indeed, between 1979 and 1989, UK manufacturing output grew by just 15 per cent – an average annual growth rate of barely 1 per cent. The recession then led output to fall steeply, so that by 1992 it had fallen back to around its 1973 level.

Some claim that manufacturing does not matter. We believe it does. Loss of jobs has been accompanied by a rising trade deficit and falling employment. This process of 'deindustrialisation' has seriously damaged our wealth. Much of the service sector depends on the manufacturing sector for its very existence.

Deindustrialisation has also created conditions in which firms cut their support for training – both internal and external. That, in turn, has weakened the local infrastructure.

Firms have also tended to switch their focus to a narrow range of specific skills to meet their immediate needs, which has made it more difficult for non-manufacturing businesses to find suitably skilled labour when they want

Abridged from The *Observer*, 21 January 1996

sector – all share this view and work together towards achieving it.

In the UK, there has been a relative absence of consensus and coordination, and the Treasury in the 1980s even claimed that there is nothing special about manufacturing and that the balance of payments is a matter of indifference. UK governments have been accused of failing to implement a coherent and ongoing industrial policy framework, while pursuing macroeconomic policies that have damaged the manufacturing base.

It has also been argued that the financial sector has too often adopted a short-term perspective in relation to investment in manufacturing, with a preference for dividend payments at the expense of ploughing back profits for investment. Among manufacturers there may have also been a tendency to regard exporting as a 'marginal activity' and to shy away from trying to penetrate the major international markets.

Conclusion

The main cause of the long-term decline of the UK manufacturing sector has been its weak trade performance. However, it is clear that it is not primarily reduced cost competitiveness that has contributed to the increased foreign penetration of British markets and gradual elimination of the UK trade surplus in manufactured goods.

In the longer term, it is non-price factors such as design, quality, marketing and other aspects of the product package that have contributed to a low income elasticity of demand for UK manufactured goods. The weak trade performance of the UK manufacturing sector has been due more to these non-price factors than simply to price uncompetitiveness, and this in turn has its roots in weak investment and R&D, and antipathy towards manufacturing adopted by the key actors in the economy.

This is not to say that price competitiveness is not important, or that it has not sometimes contributed to job losses in manufacturing. Indeed, during the 1980s and 90s, as we will see in the next chapter, the decline of manufacturing in the UK was considerably exacerbated by a loss of price competitiveness due to temporary exchange rate movements.

KEY WORDS

Production function	Balance of trade
Process innovation	Import penetration
Product innovation	Exports-to-sales ratio
Crowding out	Price competitiveness
Marketable output	Non-price factors
Non-marketable output	IMF index of relative unit labour costs
Competitiveness	Relative producer prices
North Sea oil	Income elasticity of demand
Dutch disease	Research and development

Reading list

Bacon, R. and Eltis, W., *Britain's Economic Problem Revisited,* 3rd edn, Macmillan, 1996.

Clark, A., Layard, R. and Rubin, M., *UK Unemployment,* 3rd edn, Heinemann Educational, 1997.

Essay topics

1. Examine the causes and consequences of the fall in the share of the UK's gross domestic product (GDP) accounted for by manufacturing. [100 marks]
   [University of London Examinations and Assessment Council 1994]

2. (a) What do you understand by the term 'deindustrialization'? [30 marks]
   (b) Examine the factors that have contributed to deindustrialization in the UK. [70 marks]
   [University of London Examinations and Assessment Council 1994]

3. 'In May 1993, the Swan Hunter Shipyard on Tyneside went into receivership – one fifth of the 2 200 workers lost their jobs and further redundancies are inevitable.' (*The Guardian,* 25 May 1993)
   Explain the likely reasons for this and discuss the extent to which it is a typical example of deindustrialization in the UK. [20 marks]
   [Combined boards of University of Cambridge Local Examinations Syndicate/Oxford and Cambridge Schools Examination Board 1995]

Data Response Question

This task is based on a question set by the University of London Examinations and Assessment Council in 1995. Study the data on the UK's manufacturing sector in Table A and Figure A and then answer the questions.

Table A Manufacturing and productivity in the UK (1979 = 100)

Year	Index of output in manufacturing industry	Output per person employed in manufacturing	UK manufacturing investment	Employees in manufacturing industry (thousands)
1979	100	100	100	7,107
1980	91	96	89	6,801
1981	86	99	70	6,099
1982	86	106	68	5,751
1983	89	115	67	5,418
1984	92	122	80	5,302
1985	94	125	92	5,254
1986	95	129	86	5,122
1987	101	138	91	5,049
1988	108	146	102	5,089
1989	112	152	113	5,080
1990	112	152	111	5,046

Source: *The Guardian*, 12 March 1992

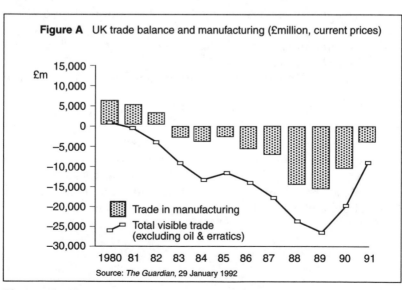

Figure A UK trade balance and manufacturing (£million, current prices)

Source: *The Guardian*, 29 January 1992

1. Between 1979 and 1990 employment in manufacturing fell by over 2 million, yet output rose by 12 per cent. How do you account for this? [3 marks]
2. Suggest *three* reasons that might explain why 'output per person employed in manufacturing' changed over this period. [9 marks]
3. Explain why the trend in 'trade in manufacturing' between 1980 and 1991 shown in Figure A would be of concern to UK policy-makers.
4. What other data would help in assessing the performance of the whole economy over the period shown? Explain your answer. [4 marks]

Chapter Five

The contraction of the manufacturing sector after 1979: a tale of two recessions

' *UK manufacturing is lean and mean, but its output is barely to be seen.*' Martin Wolf writing in the *Financial Times*

While employment in manufacturing has been on a downward trend since 1966, during the early 1980s and 90s there were particularly large reductions. There were recessions at the beginning of each decade, leading to dramatic reductions in employment and output in manufacturing. In each case, during the subsequent upturns, employment in manufacturing hardly increased.

In this chapter we shall first examine the factors that led to the contraction of the manufacturing sector at the beginning of the 1980s. We go on to consider why employment in manufacturing did not recover during the boom of the second half of the 1980s, before examining what happened to the manufacturing sector in the early 1990s, when the UK economy went into another, deep recession.

The contraction of manufacturing, 1979–82

In 1979, the Conservatives led by Mrs Thatcher were elected to power after five years of a Labour government, and the UK became a laboratory experiment for the application of the doctrine of **monetarism**. Very tight monetary and fiscal policies were pursued in order to 'squeeze inflation out of the system'.

Inflation did eventually abate, but the price was the deepest **recession** since the Great Depression of the early 1930s. The contraction of the manufacturing sector was unprecedented:

* output fell by 16 per cent;
* investment fell by over 30 per cent;
* 1.3 million jobs were lost and unemployment rose from 1.3 million to 2.8 million.

Figure 9 gives details of employment and output by sector over the period 1977–94. These indexed statistics show clearly that the contraction of manufacturing output and employment was the main feature of the recession of the early 1980s. There was some decline in employment in the services sector but this was relatively small.

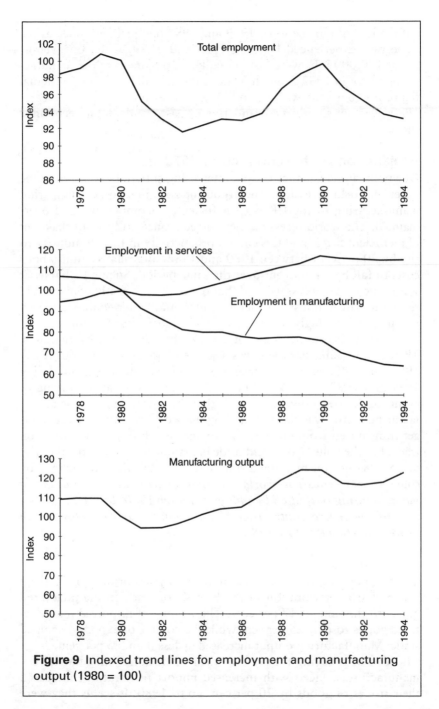

Figure 9 Indexed trend lines for employment and manufacturing output (1980 = 100)

If the loss of jobs between 1979 and 1982 had just continued at the same rate experienced between 1966 and 1979, when on average about 150 000 jobs were lost annually, employment in the manufacturing sector in 1982 would have gone down to 6.5 million. The actual figure for that year was 5.5 million, so what happened in the early 1980s was not simply a continuation of past trends but an **economic shock**.

Explanations of the contraction, 1979–82

One popular view is that UK manufacturing suffered unduly from the onset of **world recession**. The argument goes that for a long period manufacturing in the UK was inefficient, uncompetitive and over-manned. The world recession then forced a once-and-for-all shakeout of inefficient firms, and this caused productivity in British industry to rise by 20 per cent between 1980 and 1982, and relative unit labour costs to fall by 14 per cent over the same period. Such a catharsis, it was argued, was necessary, and that out of the ashes a Phoenix would rise with British industry leaner and fitter, and better equipped to survive in an increasingly competitive international environment.

This view, however, does not seem to be supported by the facts. There is no doubt that there was a severe world recession in the early 1980s. In 1980, world industrial production was stagnant, and during 1981 and 1982 it fell by 10 per cent. A close look at the timing of events in the UK, however, reveals that the contraction of the manufacturing sector was not initiated by the world recession. Recessions get transmitted from one country to another through the impact on trade, but the volume of world trade in manufactures continued to rise up to 1981 – after manufacturing output in the UK had declined by some 14 per cent. *The world recession exacerbated the decline in manufacturing output and employment after 1980, but the explanation of the severe contraction of the manufacturing sector lies in factors affecting it before 1980.*

- ### The build-up to the contraction
The first point to mention is that in the two years prior to 1979 there was a sharp deterioration in the balance of trade in manufactured goods to the tune of 17 per cent. The volume of imported manufactured goods rose by 25 per cent while the volume of exports remained static. Manufacturing output increased by less than 0.5 per cent.

Instead of reducing the *scale* of their operations immediately, UK manufacturers, faced with increased import penetration, increased their *stocks* of goods by 20 per cent up to 1980. It seems they were expecting demand to increase, but this did not happen for at least two reasons:

- the pursuit of a highly **deflationary economic policy** by the newly elected Conservative government in 1979;
- the rapid appreciation of the **exchange rate** in 1979 and 1980.

• Deflationary economic policy

The primary aim of economic policy from 1979 became the control of inflation, which showed signs of accelerating from an already high level with the collapse of incomes policy in 1978–79 under the previous Labour government.

The new Conservative government's strategy involved cutting government expenditure in order to reduce the size of the public sector borrowing requirement (PSBR), in the belief that this would help to curb the growth of the money supply from the supply side. According to monetarist doctrine, 'inflation is always and everywhere a monetary phenomenon' in a causal sense, and a sufficient condition for the control of inflation is, therefore, control of the money supply.

A **medium-term financial strategy** (MTFS) was introduced with the aim of controlling the growth of M3 money to below 10 per cent. Interest rates were raised to control the demand for money, with average short-term interest rates rising from 11.6 per cent in 1978 to 15.8 per cent in 1979, and the interest rate was kept high throughout 1981 and 1982. All this had a dramatic effect on the domestic demand for manufactured goods, particularly through the adverse impact on investment demand which declined by over 30 per cent, and consumers' expenditure which was stagnant in real terms between 1979 and 1981.

• Exchange rate appreciation

The second factor which depressed the demand for UK manufactured goods was the rapid appreciation of the exchange rate in 1979 and 1980. Against the dollar, the value of sterling rose from $1.92 in 1978 to $2.33 in 1980 – a rise of over 20 per cent. Against a basket of currencies, the value of sterling (i.e. the effective exchange rate) rose by 18 per cent over the same short period, as Figure 10 shows.

Three major factors were responsible for this excessive appreciation:

- In the late 1970s, increasing amounts of foreign exchange were being saved and earned by the production and export of North Sea oil. Between 1977 and 1979, fuel output doubled and exports increased by over 80 per cent.

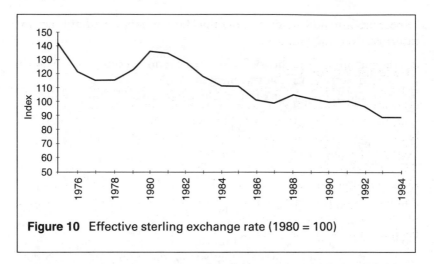

Figure 10 Effective sterling exchange rate (1980 = 100)

- High interest rates made sterling assets attractive for foreigners to hold, which added considerably to the demand for sterling.
- The recession (combined with North Sea oil) caused the balance of payments on current account to go into surplus – to the tune of £3 billion in 1980. This added to the demand for sterling relative to supply; or to look at it another way, weakened the demand for foreign currency relative to supply.

The effect of the exchange rate appreciation, however, was to switch demand from domestic to overseas suppliers of manufactured goods on a massive scale. There was a strong increase in **import penetration**, and the balance of trade surplus in manufactured goods continued to diminish – until finally in 1983 it went into deficit for the first time in British economic history.

- **The outcome**

The deflationary economic policy and the rise in the exchange rate, coupled with the world recession and the factors contributing to the long-run decline of the manufacturing sector (which we described in the previous chapter), combined to produce the huge contraction of the UK manufacturing sector in the early 1980s.

The years 1979 to 1982 were serious for manufacturing industry. Factories shut down, workers were laid off, and the number of bankruptcies and insolvencies rocketed. Certain towns and cities became unemployment blackspots because of the disappearance of major industrial employers, which in turn had downward **multiplier effects** on local economies. As firms closed down, so the capital base for any future recovery was reduced.

The legacy after 1982

After 1982, the UK economy began to recover. Total employment levels ceased to fall, thanks to the creation of jobs in the service sector. Output in manufacturing started to increase and began the long climb back to its pre-recession levels. Unemployment continued to rise, however, and peaked in 1986 at 3.3 million.

The UK experienced a **boom** from 1986 to 1989, with GDP growth rates averaging around 4 per cent, based on high consumer spending and increasing property values, and unemployment fell to 1.8 million in 1989. However, the contraction of the manufacturing sector left behind a number of problems.

• Balance of payments constraint

A worsening manufacturing trade deficit meant that, in the 1980s, the overall growth rate consistent with balance of payments equilibrium on the current account was deteriorating. To put it another way, *balance of payments deficits started to emerge sooner and quicker as growth exceeded a certain level.*

This happened with a vengeance during the recovery of the economy after 1982. The current account of the balance of payments swung from a surplus of £5 billion in 1983, to a rough balance at the beginning of 1986, and then into a deficit of £21 billion in 1989. The long-run growth rate of GDP consistent with balance of payments equilibrium appears to have fallen to no more than 2 per cent a year, compared with nearly 3 per cent in the period 1951–79.

It became fashionable in the 1980s to argue that the size of the deficit was not a cause for concern. Foreigners, it was said, are prepared to finance the current account deficit by holding UK financial assets, which create an offsetting surplus on the capital account (net of changes in reserves). *Whether this situation can be sustained depends on overseas confidence in the management and performance of the economy.* In particular, rising inflation or a currency depreciation will lead to capital losses for foreigners holding UK financial assets, unless the rate of interest in the UK is raised to compensate. Increases in domestic rates of interest, however, restrain investment, which reduces aggregate demand and undermines the future growth prospects of the economy. Interest-elastic consumer expenditures may also be reduced, which will reduce aggregate demand further.

If high interest rates are not sufficient to stave off unwanted currency depreciation – with foreigners withdrawing their capital from UK assets, causing the demand for sterling to fall – then drastic reductions in aggregate demand will be required to reduce imports and bring the current account back into equilibrium. This will, in turn, lead to higher unemployment. This is exactly what happened in the late 1980s:

- The base rate was raised from 8.5 per cent in 1987 to 15 per cent in 1989, and real interest rates were kept high in the early 1990s to protect the value of sterling within the quasi-fixed **exchange rate mechanism** (ERM) of the European Monetary System (EMS), which the UK joined in 1990.
- Unemployment in 1991 approached 2.5 million, close to the level of the severe recession of the early 1980s.

The balance of payments situation therefore does matter because the interest rate level required to protect the currency has implications for the real economy.

- **The problem of unemployment**

Unemployment was on a rising trend in the UK throughout the 1970s: in 1970 it stood at 600 000, and it had risen to 1.1 million by 1979. By 1981 it had doubled and eventually reached 3.3 million in 1986.

It fell to 1.8 million during the boom of 1986–89. Part of the recorded reduction, however, was due to fewer people claiming unemployment and related benefits, rather than fewer people actually looking for work, as a consequence of changes made to how unemployment figures are collected.

After 1989 unemployment rose again. Furthermore the proportion of **long-term unemployed** – those unemployed for more than 12 months – increased from 25 per cent in 1980 to over 40 per cent in 1989.

In spite of the arguments about the exact number of unemployed people, it is clear that the decline of the manufacturing sector in this period created an unemployment problem that is still to be cured.

If employment in the manufacturing sector continues to fall, or remains static, unemployment will only be reduced if other sectors can grow fast enough (unless the size of the labour force falls). In the period 1984–89, employment rose almost exclusively in the service sector, as Table 9 shows. In particular, sizeable increases in employment occurred in the financial services sector, in wholesale and retail distribution, and in education. Furthermore, while male employment hardly changed, female employment increased substantially by nearly 1.5 million.

Along with these changes in the industrial and gender composition of employment has been a marked increase in part-time work, defined as 30 hours or less per week. Of the 1.5 million jobs created (in net terms) between 1984 and 1989, more than half were for part-time workers.

Table 9 Changes in employment in the UK, 1984–94 (thousands)

	1984	1989	1984–89	1994	1989–94
Total employees in employment	21 238	22 756	+1 518 (+7.1%)	21 397	−1 359 (−6.0%)
Males	11 888	11 979	+91 (+0.01%)	10 786	−1 193 (−10.0%)
Females	9 350	10 776	+1 426 (+15.2%)	10 611	−165 (−1.5%)
Agriculture, forestry and fishing	340	300	−40	266	−34
Energy and water supply	616	471	−145	313	−158
Construction	1 037	1 062	+25	786	−276
Manufacturing industry	5 409	5 234	−175	4 328	−906
Service industries	13 836	15 688	+1 852	15 761	+73
of which:					
Wholesale and retail distribution	2 958	3 213	+255	3 201	−12
Hotels and catering	1 010	1 124	+114	1 228	+104
Banking, finance and insurance	1 969	2 675	+706	2 707	+32
Public administration and defence	1 602	1 650	+48	1 372	−278
Education	1 603	1 797	+194	1 901	+104
Transport and communication	1 341	1 362	+21	1 231	−131
Other services	699	892	+193	992	+100

Source: Annual Abstract of Statistics

The recession of 1990–92, and after

The rate of growth of the UK economy fell from 4.9 per cent in 1988 to 0.6 per cent in 1990, and the economy went into recession again with negative growth in 1991 and 1992. The downturn was the result of policies to curb demand and to contain inflationary pressures emanating from the housing sector.

A combination of earlier income tax cuts and lax monetary policy, coupled with soaring house prices, gave rise to a consumer-led boom, causing inflation to accelerate and the balance of payments to go into deficit.

The government's response was to tighten its monetary policy by raising interest rates to 15 per cent. This caused the rate of growth of GDP to be halved between 1988 and 1989, to come to a halt in late 1990, and to fall by more than 2 per cent in 1991. Once again unemployment soared, reaching 2.7 million in 1992.

The budget *surplus* of £12 billion in 1989 was transformed into a *deficit* of £22 billion in 1992. High interest rates were also required to maintain the parity of sterling within the European ERM.

It can be argued that once again the real economy was sacrificed on the twin crosses of containing inflation by blunt monetary instruments, and maintaining the value of sterling.

- **Further downturn of the manufacturing sector**

As Table 9 shows, in employment terms, the UK economy peaked in 1990. The number of employees in employment fell by 1.5 million, from 22.9 million to 21.4 million in 1994.

Once again employment in the manufacturing sector fell substantially. Unlike total employment, manufacturing employment had peaked in 1988 (after a small rise in 1987–88) and had fallen by 700 000 by 1992 (the trough of the cycle) and by 900 000 (or 17 per cent) by 1994.

Manufacturing output fell by 6 per cent from its peak in 1989 to a low point in 1992, and investment (in real terms) fell by 20 per cent over the same period.

There were a number of differences, however, between the recession of the early 1980s and that of the early 1990s:

- Although the exchange rate was maintained at a high level, in the framework of the ERM, it did not appreciate in the same dramatic fashion as in 1979 and 1980. There was no sudden reduction in price competitiveness due to macroeconomic policy. In fact the trade deficit in manufactured goods was *reduced* during the recession, from nearly £17 billion in 1989 to £3.6 billion in 1991, which is the opposite of what happened in the early 1980s.

- Consumer confidence collapsed. Possible reasons were the pricking of the house price bubble, high rates of interest for borrowers, rising unemployment and job insecurity. Consumer spending fell by more than 2 per cent in real terms between 1990 and 1992, having increased by more than 25 per cent in the period 1985–90. In the previous recession of 1979–82 it had held up and even rose slightly. This caused the recession of the early 1990s to be slightly longer than the recession of the early 1980s.

- **From depreciation to recovery**

In September 1992, following intense speculative pressure, the pound was withdrawn from the ERM. Its value relative to a basket of currencies had fallen by 12 per cent by 1993, and price competitiveness improved by nearly 10 per cent.

The trade deficit in manufacturing, having fallen to only £3.6 billion in 1991 owing to the recession, increased again in 1992 to £7.1 billion. The depreciation and associated improvement in price competitiveness prevented the deficit widening in the following years, in which it remained at around £7.7 billion.

Between 1992 and 1995, *exports* of manufactured goods increased by 20 per cent in volume terms, while *imports* rose by 16 per cent. Output in manufacturing, along with the economy as a whole, started growing again. The decline in employment in manufacturing slowed down and in 1995 it appears to have increased slightly. The depreciation of sterling enabled the economy to come out of recession, bringing not only improved price competitiveness but also initially lower interest rates in both real and nominal terms.

Conclusion

The period of Conservative administrations from 1979 onwards contained two recessions in which the manufacturing sector suffered severely. Manufacturing employment is now 3 million lower and output has grown by only 10 per cent (roughly half of one per cent a year). While a large number of supply-side reforms have been implemented to improve competitiveness, and even with a sizeable depreciation of sterling, the balance of trade in manufactures is still substantially in deficit.

There remains the important question of how far job creation outside the manufacturing sector could bring unemployment down to, say, one million, which might be regarded as the level of 'full

The ills of manufacturing

MARTIN WOLF

UK manufacturing is lean and mean, but its output is barely to be seen. It has managed, since 1979, to combine dynamic productivity with stagnant output. Many hoped the recovery would mark a change to this disconcerting pattern. But, after a short surge in 1993 and 1994, manufacturing is back to its habitual ways. Why has the growth of manufacturing been so disappointing? Does it matter? Can anything be done about it?

The stagnation of UK manufacturing over the past two decades has been almost total. According to an article by Michael Kitson and Jonathan Michie of Cambridge University, which appears in a stimulating symposium in the January issue of *The Economic Journal*, the total increase in manufactured output between 1973 and 1992 was a derisory 1.3 per cent. Over the same period, manufactured output rose 68.9 per cent in Japan, 68.6 per cent in Italy, 55.2 per cent in the US, 32.1 per cent in West Germany and 16.5 per cent in France.

If output growth has been astoundingly bad, productivity growth has been highly creditable. Output per person employed in UK manufacturing rose 78 per cent between the first quarter of 1979 and the end of last year.

This combination of fast productivity growth with virtually no increase in output is quite extraordinary. It has also had two inevitable consequences – job losses and declining shares of manufacturing in gross domestic product. Between the cycles of 1964–73 and 1979–89 UK employment in manufacturing declined by a third (2.5m), against only 10 per cent to 13 per cent in France and Germany (0.5m and 1.1m, respectively). Meanwhile, the share of manufacturing in GDP collapsed from 32 per cent in 1973 to 28 per cent in 1979 and 21 per cent in 1993.

Does this striking contrast between the output and productivity performance of manufacturing actually matter?

Deindustrialisation may be important for any of four reasons:

• Because manufacturing generates large benefits for the wider economy that are not fully captured by the businesses that create them;
• Because it generates jobs for particularly important segments of the population;
• Because it earns (or saves) the bulk of the foreign exchange on which the UK depends for its prosperity; and, accordingly;
• Because it largely determines GDP and overall employment, given constraints on the country's ability to finance current account deficits by borrowing abroad.

Members of Cambridge University's Keynesian band are not the only ones who believe the failure of manufacturing to expand is worrying. Mr Walter Eltis, for example, who was adviser to Mr Michael Heseltine as trade and industry secretary notes that "few can doubt that the UK would have achieved a higher GDP and a lower natural rate of unemployment if manufacturing industry had been able to win a higher share of world markets and the UK home market".

Abridged from the *Financial Times,* 14 May 1996

employment'. Taken together with the earlier argument that economic growth will be constrained by the current account of the balance of payments, the question can be rephrased as: Can the UK economy recover to – and sustain – pre-1979 employment and unemployment levels without a recovery of the manufacturing sector, in terms of its contribution to trade and its contribution to employment? We address this issue in the final chapter.

KEY WORDS

Monetarism
Recession
Economic shock
World recession
Deflationary economic
 policy
Exchange rate

Medium-term financial
 strategy
Import penetration
Multiplier effects
Boom
Exchange rate mechanism
Long-term unemployed

Reading list
Clark, A., Layard, R. and Rubin, M., *UK Unemployment* 3rd edn, Heinemann Educational, 1997.
Smith, D., *Mrs Thatcher's Economics: Her Legacy*, 2nd edn, Heinemann Educational, 1992.

Essay topics
1. How might you explain the decline in the relative importance of manufacturing industry in the UK economy since 1979? [70 marks]
 [University of London Examinations and Assessment Council 1994]
2. (a) Outline and explain the main changes in unemployment which have occurred in the United Kingdom during the last ten years. [12 marks]
 (b) Evaluate the extent to which government policies have influenced the level of unemployment. [13 marks]
 [Associated Examining Board 1996]

Data Response Question
This task is based on a question set by The University of Cambridge Local Examinations Syndicate in 1995. Read the article and study Figure 1 (adapted from *The Guardian*, 25 May 1993). Then answer the questions.

NORTH FIGHTS BACK IN SWAN'S CRISIS

The entrance to the Swan Hunter Shipyard on Tyneside has a steep slope, like a slipway. On Friday, 420 of the 2000 workers will walk down that slipway for the last time. There remains harrowing uncertainty for the remainder of one of the highest skilled manufacturing workforces in Europe.

The crisis at Swan Hunter focuses a piercing spotlight on government policy on manufacturing and sets a question mark against the stated commitment to intervention of the President of the Board of Trade, Michael Heseltine. Swan's went into receivership twelve days ago after losing a £170 m helicopter carrier order to a partnership led by VSEL, based in Barrow-in-Furness (also in the North). The threat to Swan is an indication of the radical nature of structural employment changes faced by this struggling region.

The number of jobs in Tyne and Wear is expected to rise by only 5600 (1.2%) by 2001. Sweeping changes will see an expansion in part-time, service sector and female employment as manufacturing, the region's historic bedrock, which has provided full-time jobs for men, shrinks. Forecasts suggest that the manufacturing workforce will decline by 25%, leaving it as only 15.5% of the total by 2001. Full-time employment is projected to fall by 24%; self-employment is expected to grow by 15%.

Investment by Japanese firms such as car manufacturing giant Nissan have brought new opportunities, but also potential dangers to the region. Nissan symbolizes the revival of manufacturing in the North-East, a region without a history of motor manufacturing. Production, though, this year has stalled and indicators suggest that the flow of inward Japanese investment is likely to diminish. The North-East has enjoyed less inward investment in the 1980s while, in contrast, Portugal has seen a forty-fold increase in investment from Japanese companies.

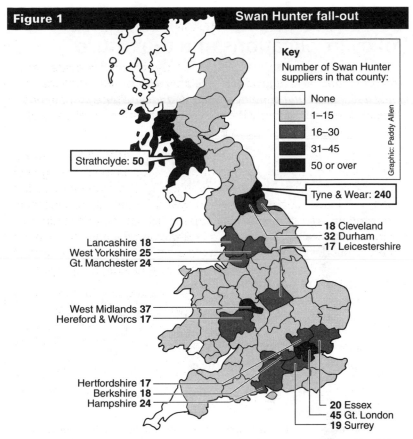

Figure 1   **Swan Hunter fall-out**

Key

Number of Swan Hunter suppliers in that county:

- None
- 1–15
- 16–30
- 31–45
- 50 or over

Graphic: Paddy Allen

Strathclyde: **50**

Tyne & Wear: **240**

18 Cleveland
32 Durham
17 Leicestershire

Lancashire **18**
West Yorkshire **25**
Gt. Manchester **24**

West Midlands **37**
Hereford & Worcs **17**

Hertfordshire **17**
Berkshire **18**
Hampshire **24**

20 Essex
45 Gt. London
19 Surrey

© M. Halsall, *North Fights Back in Swan Crisis*, adapted from *The Guardian*, 25 May 1993

1. (a) State **two** indicators of deindustrialization referred to in the article. [2 marks]
   (b) Explain why these are appropriate indicators. [2 marks]
2. In July 1994, Swan Hunter went into receivership and it was unlikely that the company could continue to operate.
   With reference to Figure 1:
   (a) How will the closure have affected Tyne and Wear? [2 marks]
   (b) Explain how the information can be applied to illustrate the multiplier process. [4 marks]
3. Use the case of Swan Hunter to explain how deindustrialization might have affected the UK's balance of payments. [4 marks]
4. Assess the costs and benefits of inward Japanese investment to a region such as Tyne and Wear which is facing deindustrialization. [6 marks]

Chapter Six

Policy implications and the future

'The competitiveness approach is an over-arching culture change which will give us higher living standards and a better quality of life.'
Michael Heseltine, formerly President of the Board of Trade

If the process of deindustrialization is to be halted, the trade performance of the manufacturing sector needs to be improved. There are three possible routes:

- improving price competitiveness;
- increasing the rate of growth of exports; or
- restricting the growth of imports.

Improving price competitiveness

It was stressed in Chapter 4 that there are two types of **competitiveness**: price and non-price. While the long-run decline of the manufacturing sector and the worsening trade balance in manufactured goods have been mainly a consequence of non-price factors, price uncompetitiveness through the exchange rate – as the experience of the early 1980s showed – can also be a key determinant of the balance of trade and has sometimes contributed to the contraction of the manufacturing sector.

It is also possible that as barriers to trade have been progressively removed and transport costs reduced, international competition on the basis of price differences has become more pertinent. Furthermore, as developing countries become increasingly capable of producing more sophisticated goods with relatively cheap labour and capital, international competition in certain products will intensify.

Price competitiveness is determined by three main factors:

- labour and other input costs;
- productivity levels;
- the exchange rate.

Supply-side policies

Measures to reduce labour costs, to increase productivity, and to improve profitability were implemented in the 1980s as part of what have come to be known as **supply-side policies**. The major policies implemented were:

- trade union reforms to improve working practices and reduce strikes;
- reductions in the marginal rate of tax to encourage enterprise and greater work effort;
- the privatization of nationalized industries to increase competition, and general deregulation of the economy to promote competition and efficiency.

These policies and reforms were aimed at increasing the capacity of the economy, to produce higher output and to increase welfare without inflationary pressures arising as aggregate demand expands. The OECD believes that the policies may have been successful in this regard. On the other hand, the UK has continued to slip down the league table of competitiveness (see the boxes on pp. 76–7). Strikes have fallen to an all-time low, which has made the UK more attractive to overseas investment (see p. 82), and loss-making nationalized industries have been replaced by some highly profitable privatized companies (e.g. British Airways and British Aerospace). But as Healey and Cook document in their book *Supply Side Economics*, there has been no acceleration in the underlying growth rate of the economy, and the productivity gains in manufacturing have come about largely through a reduction in employment rather than an expansion of output.

What the OECD thinks

If the first achievement of the Tory governments since 1979 was to stop the UK's relative economic decline, many economists identify a second that may prove of even greater significance. They claim that various reforms introduced during this period have raised the average rate at which GDP can grow over the long-run without pushing up inflation. The government has increased the trend growth rate it uses in its forecasts, and the OECD has done likewise. If this is correct, the UK may soon soar up the world prosperity league.

The OECD, among others, argues that greater labour-market flexibility resulting from Tory attacks on union privileges, reforms of labour law and tighter rules on unemployment benefits have helped to create extremely favourable conditions for creating jobs quickly (hence the early fall in unemployment in this recovery) and without pushing up inflation.

The OECD also argues that the UK has benefited in recent years from being more exposed to competitive forces than many rival economies. This is due to the creation of Europe's single market, to privatisation and deregulation, and to changes in industrial structure following the prompt adoption of new technologies.

That is largely true. However, unless the UK pursues a more vigorous anti-trust policy at home, many of these gains could evaporate.

Abridged from *The Economist*, 8 June 1996

Britain tumbles down the competition league table

PHILIP BASSETT

Competitiveness is now the principal economic watchword. So far, its pursuit by the Government has meant two large White Papers, promoted by the Prime Minister and the Cabinet's biggest hitters.

Embarrassing, then, in the face of all this focus, that Britain's competitiveness appears actually to be worsening, rather than improving. Today the annual competitiveness scoreboard is published, and Britain has slipped from 14th to 18th place. While that may well underline the severity of the problem that the focus on industrial competitiveness is supposed to be addressing, it is hardly a ringing endorsement of success.

Even worse, the findings of the World Economic Forum come only days after Mr Heseltine's former principal economic lieutenant concluded the opposite. Walter Eltis, previously head of the National Economic Development Office and the former President of the Board of Trade's chief economic adviser, praised Britain's improvement in competitiveness in a report from the Foundation for Manufacturing and Industry, a business think-tank. He said that British manufacturing had, since the Conservatives came to office in 1979, closed three-quarters of its productivity gap with Germany and France.

Some of this disagreement rests on what competitiveness, a notoriously slippery concept, actually is. The UK Government sees it as "the degree to which a country can, under free and fair market conditions, produce goods and services which meet the test of international markets, while simultaneously maintaining and expanding the real incomes of people over the long term".

For its part, the Swiss-based World Economic Forum sees competitiveness as "the ability of a country or company to, proportionately, generate more wealth than its competitors in world markets".

However slippery the definition may be, and however inadequate the statistical means by which it is described, all those engaged in the competitiveness business acknowledge that the WEF's regular scoreboard is a key benchmark – which makes the UK's slippage and current ranking all the more alarming.

Eighteenth overall in terms of world competitiveness. Fifteenth out of the 24 OECD countries. Eleventh in Europe out of 23. Second to bottom in G7, beating only Italy. While ministers like to attack those whom they see as knocking Britain, the Government – especially given its tendency to make competitiveness a fetish – will find it hard to defend such figures.

Abridged from *The Times,* 6 September 1995

Productivity in manufacturing increased by 90 per cent between 1980 and 1994, having risen by only 44 per cent in the fifteen-year period 1965-79. However, the level of productivity still lies below that of our major competitors such as Germany, France and the USA. Furthermore, while the rapid productivity gains have contributed to a reduction in costs, they have not always fed through to reductions in prices which would have improved competitiveness. Instead, they went into increased profits. *The net result is that while manufacturing*

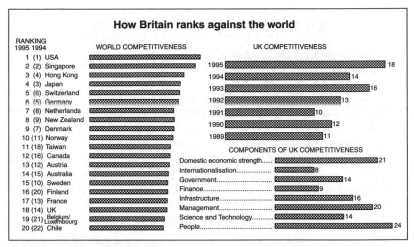

How Britain ranks against the world

RANKING
1995 1994

WORLD COMPETITIVENESS

1 (1) USA
2 (2) Singapore
3 (4) Hong Kong
4 (3) Japan
5 (6) Switzerland
6 (5) Germany
7 (8) Netherlands
8 (9) New Zealand
9 (7) Denmark
10 (11) Norway
11 (18) Taiwan
12 (16) Canada
13 (12) Austria
14 (15) Australia
15 (10) Sweden
16 (20) Finland
17 (13) France
18 (14) UK
19 (21) Belgium/Luxembourg
20 (22) Chile

UK COMPETITIVENESS

1995   18
1994   14
1993   16
1992   13
1991   10
1990   12
1989   11

COMPONENTS OF UK COMPETITIVENESS

Domestic economic strength......   21
Internationalisation...................   8
Government............................   14
Finance...................................   9
Infrastructure..........................   16
Management...........................   20
Science and Technology...........   14
People....................................   24

The Times, 6 September 1995

productivity has improved, it has done little to increase manufacturing output or improve the trade performance of the manufacturing sector.

- **Currency depreciation**

One of the major policy instruments available to improve price competitiveness is the **exchange rate.** An exchange rate depreciation will improve the balance of trade in manufactures, provided the demands for exports and imports are sufficiently price-elastic. The specific condition is that the price elasticities of demand for exports and imports sum to greater than one in absolute value (the **Marshall-Lerner Theorem**).

The effect that exchange rate depreciation has on the balance of trade, however, is also dependent on other policies being pursued at the same time, particularly with respect to monetary policy. For example, if a high-interest-rate policy is being pursued to restrict the demand for credit, this may worsen competitiveness by increasing costs and reducing investment (as well as attracting short-term capital inflows which will tend to offset the depreciation).

The relevance of exchange rate depreciation for improving competitiveness and the balance of payments in the long run can also be questioned:

- Currency depreciation tends to hamper industrial progress by making countries more competitive in the very types of goods that are responsible for their balance of payments difficulties, through the production of 'down-market' goods.
- Depreciation would have to be continuous to put a country on a

higher growth path consistent with balance of payments equilibrium.
- Depreciation can be highly inflationary since it raises the price of imported goods.

Thus, currency depreciation cannot be relied upon to improve competitiveness or to rectify balance of payments disequilibrium for a long period. This point is well illustrated by the experience of the depreciation of sterling following its exit from the ERM in September 1992. The current account of the balance of payments improved temporarily through a temporary surge in exports, but once recovery got under way the deficit widened again.

Which trade strategy is best for the UK?

Improved price competitiveness can only provide a partial solution to the weak trade performance of the UK manufacturing sector. Some form of trade strategy will be required to raise the rate of growth of exports, and to prevent further import penetration, by improving the non-price components of competitiveness.

- Protectionism

One of the major threatening positions in international trade negotiations is recourse to **protectionism**. Whether by tariffs on imported goods, or by import quotas, **import controls** are isolationist and inward-looking. While import controls may foster the substitution of domestically produced goods for imported goods, there are a number of shortcomings associated with such a strategy:
- Inefficient domestic producers are protected, and consumers pay higher prices than would otherwise be the case. A dynamic growth and development policy cannot be based on protection.
- Other countries may retaliate, which will limit export growth and hinder economic growth.
- The UK, as a member of the EU, cannot act unilaterally to restrict imports from other member countries.
- The UK, as a party to the World Trade Organization (WTO), cannot apply the kind of blanket import controls that would be required to halt import penetration.

If inter-country differences in export and import propensities are examined, it is not so much the UK's overall import propensity which looks so alarming, but the slow growth of exports compared with other countries. This, in turn, seems to have little to do with relative price differences, but with a very low income elasticity of demand for UK goods in world markets, owing mainly to the characteristics of the goods such as their design, reliability, delivery, marketing, servicing and quality in the widest sense. There is no hope of improving this fundamental weakness by means of import controls or by currency depreciation.

- **Export-led growth**

Policies to raise the income elasticity of demand for UK goods will therefore be necessary if the decline of the manufacturing sector is to be halted. This will require the development of new products, increased investment, more resources devoted to R&D by firms, and a change of emphasis at the national level towards manufacturing and exporting. In fact, no attempt has ever been made in the UK economy to develop a coherent strategy of **export-led growth**.

The primary task of economic policy in the UK must be to develop a strategy of export-led growth, based on measures to alter the allocation of investment resources and the composition of output in favour of exports. UK export performance is a function of the types of goods produced and the division of output between domestic and foreign markets. **Tax incentives** could be used to alter the structure of production and to raise export performance within the structure. The structural change required is to induce an allocation of resources in favour of technologically progressive industries producing goods with a high income elasticity of demand in world markets.

The key issue is, of course, how this change can be effected. One approach would be an **industrial strategy**, linked to a system of investment grants and allowances. These **investment incentives** could be discriminatory according to various growth criteria, in particular for the development of new products and technology.

A number of other things could be done. Exporting firms might be offered cheaper credit for investment; an attempt could be made to raise the status of marketing in firms; encouragement could be given to foreign-language training, and to finding room for engineers in the boardrooms of firms.

A number of elements in such an export-led growth strategy may violate international trading agreements. In particular, under European law, government aid that distorts competition is incompatible with the 'single market' – although France and Germany already subsidise their manufacturing industries to a much greater extent than other nations in Europe. Such a strategy could be acceptable if it were integrated into a regional-aid framework.

A basic problem is that, in one sense, any subsidy or tax concession to any activity distorts 'free competition'. On the other hand, free competition itself may affect trading conditions adversely if it means that a country languishes economically and under-utilizes its resources. In these circumstances, support for activities to achieve fuller utilization could enhance the volume of trade for all.

- **The 'Competitiveness' White Paper of 1994: a step in the right direction?**

After the 1992 General Election there appeared to be a change of attitude towards exporting in general and the role of the manufacturing sector in particular.

The Conservative government, having eschewed intervention in export promotion for 15 years in the belief that everything could be left to the free play of market forces and supply-side policies, published a White Paper on competitiveness. This announced the introduction of measures to improve the UK's trade performance. Furthermore, the government's attitude towards manufacturing also changed. The White Paper stated:

> A competitive manufacturing sector is essential for our long-term prosperity. ... Manufacturing is a major employer and a 1 per cent change in exports of manufactures would [have to] be balanced by a 3 per cent change in the exports of services.

The actual measures contained in the White Paper are limited, but they represent a first step towards an export promotion strategy – mainly through the provision of regionally-based export and innovation consultants, supported by the Department of Trade and Industry. The role of government in such a strategy is recognized, as is the key role played by the manufacturing sector of the economy.

The future

A number of developments are likely to worsen the situation in the UK over the coming years and make the need for a trade strategy all the more urgent. In Europe, further integration and the movement towards monetary union by member states will have important consequences for the UK economy. Furthermore, the emergence of developing countries with the capacity to manufacture products at a fraction of the cost in advanced industrialized countries will present serious problems for manufacturers, particularly at the lower end of the market.

- ### Britain in the European Union

The UK signed the Maastricht Treaty in February 1993, paving the way for economic and monetary union between the member nations of the EU. This followed the creation of a 'single market' on 1 January 1993, in which all barriers to trade in goods and factors of production were scheduled to be removed. The basic aim of measures to integrate Europe's economies is to reap economies of large-scale production and enhance competitiveness.

However, since joining the European Community in 1973 (now the EU), the UK has built up a substantial deficit with other member nations on both the current account and in trade in manufactured goods. *This is in line with predictions from economic theory and experience when weak countries join free trade areas or customs unions.* The gains from free trade are not equally distributed, and strong countries tend to benefit at the expense of the weak. The relative economic position of the UK has declined since joining the Community, and there is evidence that membership has tightened the balance of payments constraint on Britain's growth rate.

- ### 1992 and all that

The establishment of the single market, which entails the complete liberalization of trade and removal of all restrictions on the movement of capital and labour within the EU, strengthens the existing **centrifugal forces** by which rich regions and countries get richer and the poor get relatively poorer.

In neoclassical economic theory, labour and capital migrate so as to equalize the rewards to factors of production, so that *per capita* income levels will be equalized between regions and countries. However, this conflicts with the facts.

- When labour migrates towards prosperous regions, it brings with it its own demands – in the form of demand for local goods, the provision of local services, housing and so on – so that the demand for labour in the region *increases* as a result of the increased supply of labour brought about by migration.
- In contrast, labour demand will *fall* in the depressed region. The equalization of wages may not take place.

Likewise the location of investment depends not only on relative wage rates which determine the rate of profit between regions in this theoretical context, but also on the strength of demand. Investment is just as likely to flow to prosperous regions to which people are migrating as to depressed regions where wages may be lower.

The initial differences in the level of development between regions and/or countries do not necessarily give rise to forces which eliminate those differences. On the contrary, forces are set up which may perpetuate and even widen the differences. The operation of these forces has been called by the Swedish economist Gunnar Myrdal the **process of circular and cumulative causation**. These forces are factor mobility and free trade which lead to 'virtuous circles of growth' in strong regions and countries, and 'vicious circles of poverty' in weak regions and countries.

The establishment of the single market may therefore widen regional disparities in levels of prosperity in Europe.

One major benefit in recent years of the UK's membership of the EU has been the implantation of foreign-owned manufacturing firms, mainly from outside the EU, but not exclusively. Various factors have made the UK an attractive base for companies from the USA, Japan, South East Asia and elsewhere, compared with other EU countries:

- the English language;
- government financial assistance;
- improved industrial relations;
- low non-wage labour costs;
- relative flexibility in human resource management.

As a result, the UK now attracts nearly one-third of the EU's inward investment. The implantation of these firms, which employ around one-fifth of all employees in UK manufacturing and provide 40 per cent of exports, has helped cushion the decline of the manufacturing sector in recent years. Furthermore, it would appear that these companies are more dynamic than British-owned firms, with higher productivity and a superior investment record.

- ## Monetary union in Europe
The Maastricht Treaty set out a programme leading to the introduction of a **single currency** for the EU by the end of the century. Four 'monetary' **convergence criteria** have been specified for inclusion for the first group of countries to proceed to the introduction of a single currency:

- a budget deficit of less than 3 per cent of GDP;
- public debt of less than 60 per cent of GDP;
- long-term interest rates of no more than 2 per cent higher than those prevailing in the three countries with the lowest rates;
- an inflation rate not more than 1.5 per cent higher than the average in the three countries with the lowest rates.

Members of the ERM must also maintain their exchange rates within the narrow (2.25 per cent) bands around the central parity. In order to proceed to a single currency in 1999, a country must have been on the way to meeting these criteria by a certain date. A number of key European countries are experiencing difficulties in meeting these criteria because of slow economic growth, which tends to increase budget deficits as a proportion of GDP.

These criteria are specified in monetary terms and take no account of the state of the real economy. In particular, there is no reference to unemployment, to the growth of output and living standards, or the trade balance. *A country that locks into monetary union while suffering high unemployment and a trade deficit will have difficulties in overcoming these problems, because the exchange rate will have disappeared, and there will be no room for discretionary monetary policy and only limited scope for independent fiscal policy.*

The UK has an opt-out on the matter of meeting the convergence criteria for the first phase of monetary union. Any government needs to think carefully about joining a single currency before dealing with **structural problems** in the real economy associated with a shrunken manufacturing base and a balance of trade deficit in manufactured goods.

• North–south trade

The emergence of developing countries (the 'south') with manufacturing capability poses new important questions for all advanced industrialized countries (the 'north').

As literacy, numeracy and basic education are increasingly acquired, and as capital becomes more mobile internationally, low-wage countries are able to manufacture certain goods at a fraction of the cost of the same goods in advanced industrial countries. These developments concern mainly goods with low skill intensities, and it is likely that demand for unskilled workers in the 'north' is being reduced as a consequence.

Attempting to compete on the basis of paying lower wages and diluting working conditions is destined to fail in the long run, owing to differences in the stage of development between 'north' and 'south'. Erecting barriers to trade, as well as being contrary to international agreements, has the effect of preventing poorer countries from developing. The 'Asian Tigers' have demonstrated how targeting key types of manufactured products and developing a coherent trade strategy based on export growth can bring about rapid economic growth.

All this means that unless the industrialized countries can maintain technological superiority or erect barriers to trade, manufacturers in the 'north' will need to alter the structure of production towards more skill-intensive products. This will require a movement 'up-market' by firms, with appropriate investments in technology, and in physical and human capital. The increased competition emanating from newly industrialized countries underlines the need to rectify the UK's weak trade performance.

Conclusion

If the UK is to prosper, the causes and consequences of deindustrialization need to be addressed. Above all, this requires a drastic improvement in the trade performance of the manufacturing sector in order to increase export growth and limit import penetration.

One solution is to alter the structure of manufacturing output towards producing goods with high income elasticities of demand in world markets, and to place a much higher priority on exporting at all levels. This transformation will require substantial investment by firms, and ongoing support from government and financial institutions.

KEY WORDS

Competitiveness	Industrial strategy
Supply-side policies	Investment incentives
Exchange rate	Process of circular and
Marshall–Lerner Theorem	cumulative causation
Protectionism	Single currency
Import controls	Convergence criteria
Export-led growth	Structural problems
Tax incentives	

Reading list

Healey, N. and Cook, M., *Supply Side Economics,* 3rd edn, Heinemann Educational, 1996.

Smith, D., *UK Current Economic Policy*, Heinemann Educational, 1994.

Essay topics

1. (a) Describe how the UK's recent experience of deindustrialization compares with that of other countries. [10 marks]
   (b) Discuss the impact of the UK's membership of the European Community/Union on manufacturing industry in the UK. [10 marks]
   [University of Cambridge Local Examinations Syndicate 1997]
2. 'Foreign investment in British manufacturing has eliminated the problem of deindustrialization.' Discuss.
   [Oxford & Cambridge Schools Examination Board, 1996]

Data Response Question

This task is based on a question set by the University of Cambridge Local Examinations Syndicate in 1996. Read the article below, which is adapted from 'One last chance for manufacturing' by Simon Beavis, published in *The Guardian* on 29 April 1994. Also study Figure A, and then answer the questions.

MPs call for action on training and investment

The government was yesterday urged to seize an "unprecedented" but "temporary" opportunity to restore the international standing of British manufacturing, but was warned by an all-party committee of MPs that failure to do so could lead to terminal decline.

The MPs said that there were "alarming aspects" in UK manufacturing, notably the continuing low level of productivity, where UK firms lag behind their French rivals by 25 per cent, German companies by 30 per cent and US and Japanese rivals by 34 and 65 per cent. They also criticised "the remaining deep-rooted

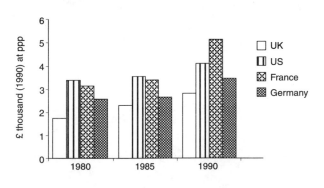

Investment per employee in manufacturing

---

problems in areas such as investment, finance for industry, training, and the rarity of strategic alliances between firms".

The MPs pinpointed the UK's slide into a rapidly growing manufacturing trade deficit, its relatively low rates of return on capital in manufacturing, low standards of management and its "exceptionally weak" medium-sized company sector. But they argued that restoring manufacturing's fortunes was essential, because it accounted for 60 per cent of exports, even though it represented only 20 per cent of GDP, because service companies often depended on manufacturers and because service companies would face an impossible task in correcting the trade deficit.

Dividend payout ratio (per cent)				
	1982	1984	1986	1988
UK	26.5	24.5	31.3	34.5
Germany	15.0	10.9	11.3	17.6

In the 146-page report, the MPs criticised financial institutions for demanding consistent dividend payouts irrespective of economic conditions, and warned that high dividends act to discourage investments which might lower profits in the short term. Warning that this places the UK at a distinct competitive disadvantage, they added: "What is required is consistent investment rather than consistent dividends."

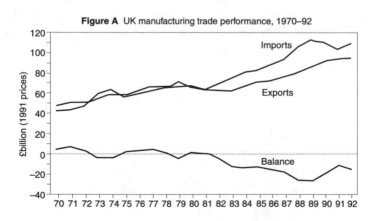

Figure A UK manufacturing trade performance, 1970–92

1. With reference to Figure A, explain how changes in the relationship between imports and exports have led to a 'rapidly growing manufacturing trade deficit.' [2 marks]
2. What is meant by the term 'low level of productivity?' [3 marks]
3. (a) In which country did manufacturing investment per employee increase most between 1980 and 1990? [1 mark]
   (b) State and explain *two* benefits of this for the economy of this particular country. [4 marks]
4. With reference to the text and data provided, explain why the UK's level of productivity in manufacturing is lower than its rivals. [4 marks]
5. In the light of the article and accompanying data, comment upon any *two* policy measures which the government might take to restore the international standing of British manufacturing. [6 marks]

Conclusion

There is no need for a long conclusion to such a short book, but we hope it has set you thinking about the UK's long-run future as a declining industrial nation, and the prospects for the growth of living standards if industrial decline continues at the same rate in the future as during the last 30 years.

In Chapter 1 we pointed out that countries go through different stages of growth in the course of their economic history, and it is natural that the share of resources devoted to industrial goods should first rise and then fall as resources switch out of agriculture in the early stages of development and into service activities in the later stages. This is associated with different income elasticities of demand for output. In this sense deindustrialization is a natural phenomenon, but it can be of the positive or negative variety.

There are many countries where deindustrialization, as defined above, has been accompanied by a fast rate of growth of GDP and expanding employment in manufacturing industry – positive deindustrialization. In other countries, including the UK, it has been accompanied by slow growth and falling manufacturing employment – negative deindustrialization.

If deindustrialization is defined, as we prefer, as the absolute decline in the number of people employed in manufacturing, resulting from slow output growth relative to productivity growth, we see that the UK has suffered a deindustrialization process in the last 30 years more severe than any other country in the world. Superimposed on the underlying downward trend have also been marked cyclical declines, particularly in the early 1980s and 90s.

We have argued in Chapter 3 that this process has serious implications for all the macroeconomic goals of full employment, balance of payments equilibrium, and rapidly rising living standards.

There is a limit to which service employment can compensate for the decline in manufacturing – partly because many service activities depend on manufacturing. There is a limit to which exports of services can compensate for a deteriorating balance of trade in manufactures, because many service activities are non-tradeable. Moreover, as far as economic growth is concerned, large-scale manufacturing activities have growth characteristics that many service activities do not possess because the latter are provided on a small scale and cannot reap increasing returns.

In Chapter 4 we discussed some of the possible causes of the deindustrialization process. We dismissed the technical progress argument, and the crowding-out hypothesis of Bacon and Eltis. The rise in the exchange rate at the time of maximum revenue from North Sea oil did wreak havoc on manufacturing industry, and did permanent damage, but the deindustrialization process started long before 1980.

Our preferred explanation of the deindustrialization of the UK is the neglect of the manufacturing sector manifested by under-investment in the sector relative to other industrialized countries, and the lack of attention to the non-price characteristics of goods which are the major determinants of demand for goods in the tradeable goods sector.

Ultimately, deindustrialization must be ascribed to the weakness of exports relative to the propensity to import, which has constrained the UK's growth rate to an average of less than 2 per cent a year since the mid-1960s, which at the same time has constrained the growth of manufacturing output. There has been a vicious circle at work of low growth, under-investment, weak R&D, poor characteristics of goods, slow export growth, leading to slow overall growth, and so on.

The situation has not been helped by the macroeconomic policy mistakes made by successive governments in the last 25 years or so, when in the 1970s economic policy-making was virtually handed over to the trade unions and the IMF, and in the 1980s and 90s errors of judgement were made:

- The tightening of monetary and fiscal policy in the early 1980s (at the time of North Sea oil) which was too severe.
- The late 1980s boom which was allowed to get seriously out of hand and was exacerbated by tax cuts.
- Entry into the ERM in 1990 at an overvalued rate relative to the deutschmark (and associated high interest rates) which caused the deepest recession since the great depression between the two world wars.

The damaging effects of these misjudgements have dwarfed the supply-side improvements associated with privatization, tax policy and trade union reform. It is certainly true that manufacturing productivity has risen, but unfortunately this was not the consequence of fast-rising output relative to employment growth, but fast-falling employment relative to virtually stagnant output growth. A country cannot thrive economically in these circumstances.

Our view is that much greater attention needs to be
formance of the tradeable goods sector; otherwise, tl
always hit the brick wall of a balance of payments co
put growth.

There is little evidence that increasing integration
Europe since joining the EU in 1973 has improved tl
ing economic performance. If anything, the rest of E
at the expense of the UK. Europe is extremely impor
trade, but the primary task must be for the country t
export-led growth strategy embracing the whole wo
growth can provide the foreign exchange for all t
nents of demand – consumption, government exp
ment – to be able to grow without balance of pa
emerging.

The Department of Trade
and Industry shows signs of
recognizing the nature of
the problem, and is now
introducing various new
measures to promote
British goods and services
abroad. At the end of the
day, however, the only way
a country will be able to
compete in world markets
is by investment and the
application of R&D to the
production of goods that
the world wants to buy.
Deindustrialization can
seriously damage a coun-
try's wealth and has been
allowed to do so now for a
number of years.

In Chapter 4 we discussed some of the possible causes of the deindustrialization process. We dismissed the technical progress argument, and the crowding-out hypothesis of Bacon and Eltis. The rise in the exchange rate at the time of maximum revenue from North Sea oil did wreak havoc on manufacturing industry, and did permanent damage, but the deindustrialization process started long before 1980.

Our preferred explanation of the deindustrialization of the UK is the neglect of the manufacturing sector manifested by under-investment in the sector relative to other industrialized countries, and the lack of attention to the non-price characteristics of goods which are the major determinants of demand for goods in the tradeable goods sector.

Ultimately, deindustrialization must be ascribed to the weakness of exports relative to the propensity to import, which has constrained the UK's growth rate to an average of less than 2 per cent a year since the mid-1960s, which at the same time has constrained the growth of manufacturing output. There has been a vicious circle at work of low growth, under-investment, weak R&D, poor characteristics of goods, slow export growth, leading to slow overall growth, and so on.

The situation has not been helped by the macroeconomic policy mistakes made by successive governments in the last 25 years or so, when in the 1970s economic policy-making was virtually handed over to the trade unions and the IMF, and in the 1980s and 90s errors of judgement were made:

- The tightening of monetary and fiscal policy in the early 1980s (at the time of North Sea oil) which was too severe.
- The late 1980s boom which was allowed to get seriously out of hand and was exacerbated by tax cuts.
- Entry into the ERM in 1990 at an overvalued rate relative to the deutschmark (and associated high interest rates) which caused the deepest recession since the great depression between the two world wars.

The damaging effects of these misjudgements have dwarfed the supply-side improvements associated with privatization, tax policy and trade union reform. It is certainly true that manufacturing productivity has risen, but unfortunately this was not the consequence of fast-rising output relative to employment growth, but fast-falling employment relative to virtually stagnant output growth. A country cannot thrive economically in these circumstances.

Our view is that much greater attention needs to be paid to the performance of the tradeable goods sector; otherwise, the economy will always hit the brick wall of a balance of payments constraint on output growth.

There is little evidence that increasing integration with the rest of Europe since joining the EU in 1973 has improved the UK's underlying economic performance. If anything, the rest of Europe has gained at the expense of the UK. Europe is extremely important for the UK's trade, but the primary task must be for the country to gear itself to an export-led growth strategy embracing the whole world. Only export growth can provide the foreign exchange for all the other components of demand – consumption, government expenditure, investment – to be able to grow without balance of payments problems emerging.

The Department of Trade and Industry shows signs of recognizing the nature of the problem, and is now introducing various new measures to promote British goods and services abroad. At the end of the day, however, the only way a country will be able to compete in world markets is by investment and the application of R&D to the production of goods that the world wants to buy. Deindustrialization can seriously damage a country's wealth and has been allowed to do so now for a number of years.